A GIFT TO MY 7 YEAR-OLD SELF

MODERN ART OF WAR

By Yaser Rashidi

MODERN ART OF WAR
TABLE OF CONTENTS

MODERN ART OF WAR
INTRODUCTION

Chess games are not won by the better tactician or the person who can think more moves ahead; the person who makes sound, calculated and accurate decisions in less time almost always wins. There's a lot of decision making in a chess game and these decisions are not necessarily about the moves, but also decisions about time management, decision about whether it's a good time to attack, defend or just make an ok move; Decisions about which side of the board to play, decision about a sacrifice and whether it's a sound or unsound sacrifice, decision about concealing your intention with a decoy move. If you can make these decisions more accurately in less time than your opponent, you'll win.

Over the years of going through my life, I have found astonishing resemblances between life situations and chess positions. I believe looking at life and chess from this point of view helps me make better decisions. In real life situations when I don't know what to do, but need to find a rule of thumb that I can use to make a decision in a short time, I go back to the rules in this book. This is the essence of all the rules boiled down into a book and it works for both chess and life as both can be modeled as strategic games. This book covers the necessary rules which are sufficient to play the perfect chess game. The rules of winning in chess and life are here in this book, you need to first play your games on this strategic level and second, observe these rules as best as possible to win more situations and positions. These rules are common between humans and computers, meaning that the best chess engines nowadays are also following the same principles as the basic rules of winning in a strategic game like life and chess are similar.

In certain chess positions, you may not see the whole line and don't have time or visualization skill to calculate and evaluate correctly, but you need to make a decision soon. To make that decision you need an intuition, a heuristic or a simplified rule to fall back onto. These are those rules of thumb. If you live your life like this, it's definitely going to be successful, but this is easier said than done. You realize this when reviewing your games and seeing the blunders, mistakes or inaccuracies. When a blunder, mistake or inaccuracy occurs it is almost always because of not observing the rules in this book. This book covers the strategy, apart from the fundamental rules in this book you only need to work on your tactics (chess puzzles). This is the route to get to your highest potential in the least amount of time.

> *"I used to attack because it was the only thing I knew. Now I attack because I know it works."*
>
> — *Garry Kasparov*

This book describes the mentality that if you follow and choose your moves aligned with this mentality, you'll win a chess game. You have to assume the role of commander of an army and what you say the army will follow. Each army consists of the queen, rooks, bishops, knights and pawns protecting the king. Kings are in the middle at the start for both sides, but after development of knights first and then bishops, king may be able to castle. Castle is an important move of the game. Castle is the only move which 2 chess pieces move at the same time. All the other moves only one piece can or can not move. Castle is intended to tuck the king on one side of the board-preferrably with pawns in front of the king protecting it. Castle is a defensive move and it's committing your king to that side of the board. If the opponent can successfully attack your castled king, you might not survive. Castle also has a positive bi-product: It brings the rook into play. Long castle can be a very strong move because it brings the rook in a central d-file. In castle short, however, you need to move the rook one more time to bring it into a central e-file. So it can be said that castle long is a tempo shorther(better) than castle short. You need to develop your army into meaningful squares and get ahead of the opponent. The mentality of that army commander is described in this book.

Magnus Carlson, the reigning world chess champion since 2013 (as of 2023), was asked: "How do you win so many games? How do you do it?" he answered with "I don't know, maybe when I get older I'll be wiser to know how I do it". He may not know it, but it is his mentality that wins the game. The mentality of resilience, fighting back, attacking on the soonest possible opportunity, not wasting time and resources, adding pressure and making calculated sacrifices when the opportunity arises. The same mentality that is described in this book. If you want to be successful and get ahead of competition, you have to pressure your mind to calculate lines, visualize and evaluate positions, and make sound judgments and moves, as quickly as possible consistently, all the time.

This mentality is so important that Magnus has a pre-game routine which he meticulously adjusts his pieces on the board. His signature move is adjusting his knights to face each other, which he does to put himself into the correct mentality. Other athletes also have pre-game routines, which are known tools to put yourself into flow state, on demand. Rafael Nadal has a specific order of his bottles that he drinks from before each game. It's his routine of putting himself into the correct mentality that wins him game after game. The reason most humans lose their game is because of wrong mentality. If you correct the mentality, you will find the strong moves in each position and over time get stronger in tactics too, because you will start to enjoy the art of calculation.

In chess, just like in life, you have to take chances and make sound sacrifices when justified. If you don't take the chance when it's time, it's like taking a hit.

If you are used to making unsound sacrifices, losing material and hoping for your opponent to make a blunder, that's your problem and you have to work on not making mistakes.

Wasting resources is bad; material is a resource and should only be sacrificed if it yields an advantage. However initiative is more important than material. The most precious resource in life and chess is time. You must be as efficient as possible. Don't get complacent. If you know the move, play it.

If you have the chance to make a sound sacrifice and don't use it, it's a form of concession; You will be pushed back into a disadvantageous position. If you have a chance to get ahead, you must find it and take that chance. Not taking a chance to get ahead is like losing material or being forced into a worse position. You have to be aggressive, opportunistic, looking for weaknesses everywhere and if you can't find any weakness, instead find moves to encourage or force your opponent to make mistakes and concessions and then think deeply on their bad and inaccurate moves, gain advantage and win the game.

I think chess is taught wrongly, especially to kids. The current method of teaching chess focuses on material, which is a pitfall of humans in both chess and life. The spirit of the chess game is not aligned with material thinking, it is rather aligned with positional advantage and initiative. Even if you're down materially you can and should come back by dynamic play and accurate moves. Initiative and positional advantage always prevails over material.

This book is about the obvious reasons that most humans lose the game. Read this book as if it's the only rules that you need. Apart from MAoW you will only need to sharpen your tactics. This is a big claim, but I think what I have written is the first time anyone claims they came up with necessary and sufficient rules governing the mindset to win in chess games. The rules in this book create a coherent mentality that will lead to thinking better and getting better at chess and also life. The rules are analogous and I have provided the same principle in life in most cases.

The order at which you learn chess concepts is very important and has a great effect on your habits and results. This is why this book is a great gift to give to a teenager, to help them not to fall into the pitfall of thinking materialistically. Many people play chess materialistically, which is the wrong mentality to have. This happens because of the way we teach chess to kids, as one of the first things you learn is the value of pieces. Material is of secondary importance, most important is the position on the board and activity of your pieces. One should be taught chess with the correct mentality, don't let material thinking get in the way of your progress. After learning how the pieces move, you should learn the most important set of rules that govern a sound playing game, which are described in this book. None of the books I've read teaches chess like this. This is how I would have liked to be taught chess at a young age. I believe teaching chess like this is closer to the spirit of this game and helps develop good habits for both chess and life.

The set of rules that govern a well played chess game are:

1. **Time management is of utmost importance.** Use time wisely, it's a scarce resource both in life and chess. If you know the next move, play it already. Don't spend time on any move more than required. Be as efficient as you can and save time, you're going to need it later. Don't get complacent. Learn to find a "good" move and make it and don't waste a lot of time on any single move, unless it's a critical move worth spending the time and analyzing deeper. Also, assign enough time to each move and don't make any hasty moves. How you and your opponent manage time has a great effect on the decisions you make and the result. If you run into time trouble, you'll be forced to make hasty moves hence blundering the game.

2. **The aim is to always have a superior position to your opponent.** This can come in many forms: tactical , strategic, material or positional advantages. At any given moment you need to know who is ahead or behind in each aspect of the game then plan and act accordingly. If you attack when it's time to attack, defend when it's time to defend and make an ok move when it's time, you'll win the game. Superior position comes from developing your pieces into meaningful squares so they work coordinated with each other.

3. **It's all about the moves and position on the board.** If you have a superior position, use it to checkmate your opponent. Moves count and nothing else.

4. **Initiative is more important than material advantage.** Although the side that has material advantage is normally expected to win, initiative almost always triumphs over material. One is expected to convert a material advantage to a win unless the other side can counter-attack and balance the position or even get a better position.

5. **Piece's nominal values are queen: 9 points , rook: 5 points, bishop: 3 points, knight: 3 points, pawn: 1 point.** These nominal values could be different based on their placement on the board and amount of activity and control they have. A well placed knight can have a value of 4 or 5 if placed on a critical square. Sometimes a single pawn can be an extremely important piece, if placed correctly.

6. **If you have options to attack and add pressure on your opponent's king, don't trade down material**, i.e., don't go into exchanges. Trading down reduces your advantage and enhances your opponent's chances of a counter attack. You need pieces to coordinate an attack and to put pressure on the position. On the other hand, there are times that trading down is good for you because it simplifies the situation and gives you an easy end-game (e.g. When you are materially ahead and an easy end-game is accessible by trading down and simplifying the position). Knowing when to trade a piece or not is super important. Knowing when an exchange is in your favor or against it is critical.

7. **You have to think about the end-position at the end of each line and evaluate it, all the time.** Visualizing the end position at the end of each line and being able to evaluate it correctly is the best skill to have in chess and in life. This is where most of the calculation happens. In old chess teaching a sound like "Tac" have always used to calculate checks and captures. Move the pieces in your mind and each time a capture or check happens say Tac. Tac is similar to sound of sword to iron of the armor. Using this sound helps you calculate lines better in your head.

8. **You should mimic how a wise old man would act in that situation.** Someone who is always in a hurry, able to come up with a quick plan and he's almost always right because he's seen all the tricks and knows what he wants in each situation. They play accurate moves even if they're down material and try to beat you in other possible

ways. They always make acceptable moves even if all they have is a few seconds. They may not find the absolute best move at times, but they think enough to not make a blunder or mistakes, ALL THE TIME.

9. **Correct evaluation of the position and making sound judgments and moving quickly are the best skills to have in life and chess.** Play chess like this and you'll get to your highest potential, it's a lot higher than what you think. Live life like this and you'll have fewer moments of embarrassment and get to your highest deserved positions.

   I've seen people in online games that when they are behind in material, try to "win on time". It means they try to make sound moves very quickly and put their opponent under time pressure and win an otherwise lost game just by better time management.

   Knowing that you have to always make sound judgments in the least amount of time is the essence of success. You could be behind in material, but using sound judgements, assigning enough time to all moves, trying to find weaknesses for both sides and taking advantage of them, trying to equalize and counter-attack, grinding the opponent until they give up is the mindset to have. If you find the move that fits this mindset perfectly, you almost always have found the best strongest move. There is almost always a best move and it's your duty to find it, on every single move.

10. **It's important to not let previous calculations interfere with new positions which emerge on the board.** Some ideas may not have been valid in the past, but that plan may become valid now. Also a plan which was valid before may become invalid with the moves played. You have to recalculate all the critical lines on every move. No easy way around it, it's hard but fruitful. Also there's no way out of it, this is the only way to get better and you have to force yourself to recalculate and re-check previous plans and threats.

Many human traits work against us in chess and life. This book shows us how to overcome that. If you stop yourself from sabotaging your position, it goes a long way in making better decisions and winning more and being more successful. The opposite is also true about your opponent: it is your duty to find bad decisions and inaccurate moves by your opponent and punish them in the best way as quickly as possible. The balance between the two sides is very fragile and it is your duty to always look and find the strongest move in the position, raise above your mind limitations and calculate more lines and evaluate the positions better. Eventually you'll get ahead by playing solid moves or by your opponent making mistakes and concessions.

Success is an objective measurable parameter in both life and Chess. There's always a best move, a 2nd best move and then a couple of ok moves and then there's a list of obvious or non-obvious inaccuracies, mistakes and then blunders. Then aim is to have less negatives and more of the positives on each move, *i.e.* finding the best move or a move which is closest to best move in terms of accuracy. If you don't manage to find the best move, It's better to find the 2nd best move rather than 3rd best move.

11. **There is only one rule that works 100% of the time: Checkmate your opponent's king.** If you have the chance to checkmate or a chance to create a checkmate threat you must do it. If you still can't, work your way up to a point that you can, by improving your position.

Below are some examples of sequences of things that can happen in a game. Here's a couple of scenarios:

Scenario 1: Opening was balanced and the middle-game resulting from it shows no clear advantage for any side. White started an attack on the king-side that black defended successfully, and the end-game was balanced too. Black made sound moves, while white over extended a pawn which eventually got captured. In the end-game, black managed to trade down everything and make that 1 extra pawn the winning pawn of the game. During the end-game, black had one chance to equalize by taking the opposition and forcing a draw, but black didn't find the only move that defended the position, and then lost the end-game.

It's very important to think of the game as a sequence of events like above. Some lines are more forceful (especially the ones with checks, captures or threats), and the end position of those lines should be calculated and planned for.

Scenario 2: White made a pawn sacrifice in the opening which caused him to lose control of the center. Black used this opportunity to make a strong pawn center which then utilized to push forward and fork a knight and bishop which resulted in black being a knight down for the rest of the game. The end game was successfully converted by black.

Scenario 3: White used an opening trick and offered a free pawn to then capture black's dark square bishop with a trick. Black didn't see the tactic, fell for the trap, and lost a bishop. White then used the material advantage to build a strong attack in the center against the exposed black king, which quickly resulted in black blundering into checkmate.

Scenario 4: The opening and middle game were balanced, with both sides playing well. In the end-game, black made a positional sacrifice to create a very strong pawn which couldn't be captured by white. Black used the space advantage and checkmated the white king against the fact that black was behind in material.

Scenario 5: The opening was played badly by both sides, with neither side taking advantage of the opponent's mistakes. In the middle game, white made a mistake which resulted in black having a strong attack against white's king. To escape the checkmate, white had to sacrifice a rook for a bishop, but then took advantage of the other rook and utilized an open file to equalize the position, infiltrate with the rook into enemy territory, and easily target the pawns. In the resulting end-game, white placed a very strong knight in a central outpost that caused him to limit the movement of black bishop, so it was a good knight - bad bishop scenario, eventually suffocating black into a checkmate position. This forced black to lose his queen for a rook, and then lose the resulting end-game.

This is a short synopsis of every game at a strategic level, and it shows you are aware of the position; whether you're ahead or behind, attacking or being attacked. This evaluation includes the phase of the game (opening, middle game, end-game). It determines your decisions, moves and resource assignment to each move. Chess should be played on this level first, and only then on the positional and tactical level. You must know at any given time who is ahead or behind: What are the advantages of each side's position? Are you attacking or under attack? What's your overall plan, what are the options and what are your threats and what to do? What are your opponent's threats? Are they behind in development or have a discoordinated army? How about yourself? What are the weaknesses? Is there a way to force or encourage your opponent to make a weakening move? If you're not playing your games on this level, you're playing chess wrong. Let go of all the puzzles, opening and tactics. You must learn and think about chess positions and be able to analyze any game from this perspective. The correct way of thinking will result in the correct way of making decisions and playing. This is a way of "Evaluation based decision making" using the least amount of resources. If you evaluate moves and lines correctly and base decisions on those calculations and evaluations while using the least amount of time, you're going to win in chess and in life.

Normally, the side with initiative has better chances than being materially ahead. It's very important to know this. Activity triumphs material, period. In chess, and in life.

Resource management is of utmost importance. No matter what your position is, it is your duty to find the best and most accurate moves or as close to it as possible in the least amount of time using the least amount of brain power. If you make a blunder, you've wasted all previous good moves, so it's important to not make blunders and minimize mistakes to as low as possible. Inaccuracies however, do happen and that's where the game is mostly played, both sides make mistakes and the side that detects and exploits the other sides' mistake will win.

When two strong players face each other, it all comes down to who plays the first inaccuracy and more often than not the side who makes the inaccuracy or mistake will pay the price for it by losing the game, unless they can find their way back or the opponent makes worse mistakes which we can utilize and equalize. It is also your duty to monitor and analyze the opponent's moves and plans on each step and detect if it's a blunder, mistake or inaccuracy and act on it. Inaccuracies, mistakes and blunders must be punished in the harshest possible way as soon as possible. Your moves must always be the most powerful move that drives the opponent to an early quit or resignation. When you're ahead and clearly winning the game, no negligence is acceptable and we must play the most strong sequence of moves that wins the game in the least amount of moves. If there's a quicker checkmate, you must choose that line against a longer line, because in the longer line your opponent may find a resource to counter back and change the equation. Being efficient is critical.

Knowing this mindset and acting on it on every move is the key to success. Knowing the patterns, tactics and puzzles is also skills of the game, but comes second after the strategic level.

It is important to know and be comfortable playing neutral positions where the game is balanced and neither side has a clear advantage. In these positions you're expected to waste no time and find a good move or if not an OK move and move on and not waste a lot of time on it while keeping the position neutral, i.e. no blunders (losing >4 points) or mistakes (losing 1~3 points).

In critical positions, there could be very few moves that can defend a position or can get an advantage out of it. You must first find the critical positions-not waste time on non-critical moves- and then spend enough time on the critical position to find the only move that's going to keep your advantage or defend a position correctly. This is still better than not having an option. In certain situations any move is bad for one side, this is called zugzwang and it is a very important concept to learn and master. If you can force the opponent into a position where every move is bad for them, it shows you have a superior position.

Abundance of choice/options is also a very good sign that you're playing well and your position is superior; the concept of double attack is derived from the same concept. If you have a lot of ways to keep your superior position and add pressure to the position it shows how strong your position is. On the other hand, if your options are limited it shows your position is under pressure. A good example of this is when one of your pieces is getting trapped and has limited (or no) option to come back to safety, or it's fine for now but if you don't do something about it, it can get trapped on the next move. This is a sign of a bad position. If you are forced to exchange one of your pieces for a lower value piece-for example forced to exchange a knight for only a pawn- it's a sign of a weak position. If one of the lines ahead gets you almost checkmated, it's a sign of a weak position.

Apart from the position on the board there are out-of-the-board factors as well, things like: How is the time situation? Is it a critical position? What are the long term plans and threats for both sides? Can they find it?

If you're playing a chess game on the tactical level only, you're on the wrong path. You must learn what's off the board and manage it properly: Time management is a very complex concept, because knowing or guessing which move is the critical position of the game and assigning enough time to it, is of utmost importance. Sometimes a grandmaster spends half of their time on one single move because they know it's the critical move of the game, and it's possible to get ahead by making a strong move next to exploit the weakness of the opponent's position.

A strong grandmaster uses disguise in their moves, meaning they play a seemingly innocent move which later turns out to be deadly. Or they decide to sacrifice their rook for a bishop, but for a much better position and chances to win the game despite being materially lower. There are many ways to play and win in chess and life. I've seen people get ahead by just playing confusingly, being unpredictable is a very important trait to have.

Learning your opponent's style of play has a strong effect on the way one plays chess. Knowing their style, usual mistakes and blindspots provides a lot of opportunities to exploit them. These are all off-the-board play and very important to know and master, along with being able to calculate lines and evaluate positions. You don't have to always find the best moves — you just have to be better than your opponent.

The rules of playing a chess game are so simple, yet the game itself is so complex. I've found similarities between chess and Life to be fascinating. They are very similar in many aspects, and I use the following rules in both.

CHAPTER 1

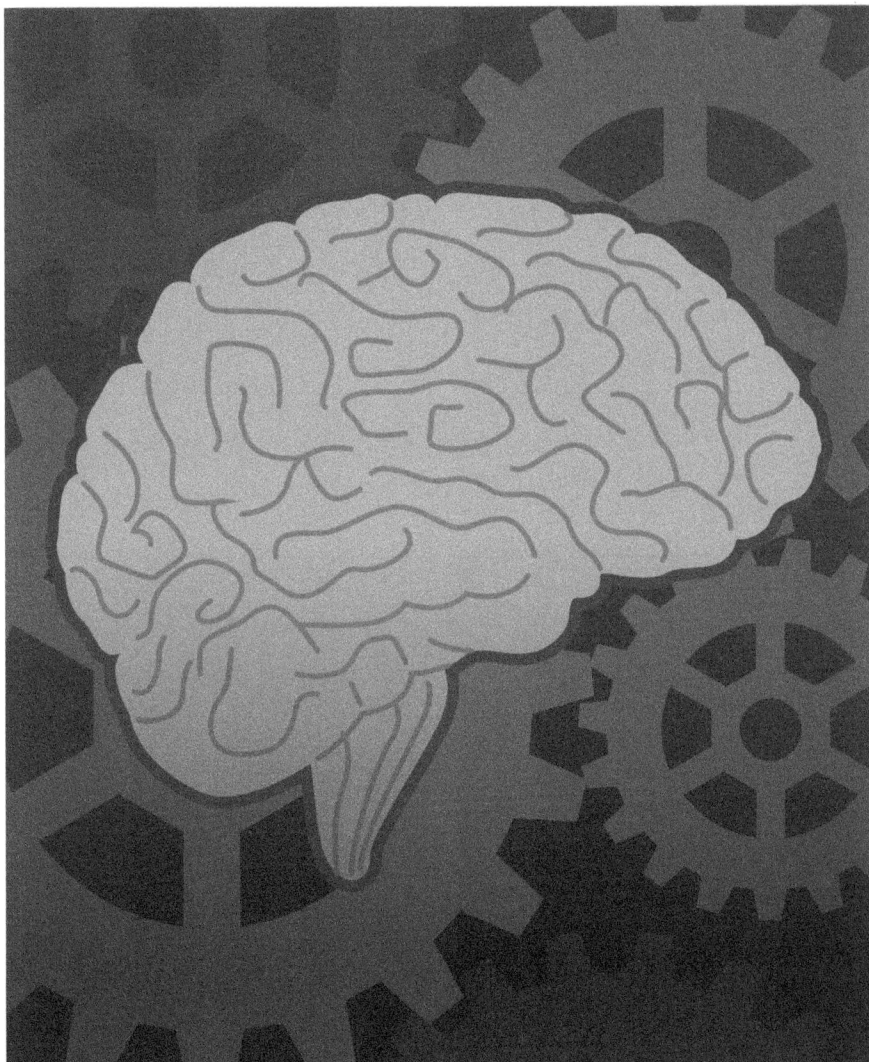

RATIONAL THINKING

CHAPTER 1
RATIONAL THINKING

The main and key skill to have is "Evaluation". This means analyzing and evaluating a position and deciding if it's neutral or if one side has a slight or decisive advantage. Correctly analyzing a position and evaluating it in comparison to other positions is the key to better decision-making, hence a better result.

It's important to note there is a measurable and objective way of evaluating each position, so always there is the best move and then 2nd best move and so on. The aim is to choose the best move or closer to best in each position in the least amount of time, consistently.

LIFE PRINCIPLE #1

Evaluating each situation correctly and acting the best in each situation is the key to success.

Position! It's all about the position on the board. Your opponent may be able to checkmate you in the next move, but if you can checkmate sooner, you're the winner. Your opponent may be 2 queens ahead in material, but if the position dictates that your remaining pieces can deliver a forcing line and checkmate their king, that material advantage is of no use. It's all about the position and whether you can find and exploit the weaknesses in it, or not.

Material plays some role and if one side is materially ahead, they are normally expected to win. However, it happens that sometimes despite being materially behind, there could be potential in the position to equalize, get ahead or even checkmate against the material odds. Material and initiative have a tricky balance and many times after a material loss there are chances for the side that lost material to equalize (right after the loss) or use a trick to gain the material back. The window of this equalizing chance is usually very short, so it's important to think very well after losing a piece and not make hasty decisions. This is also true after the opponent makes a sacrifice.

On the other hand, most of the time if you get behind in initiative, giving back some material can change the position into your favor again. If you feel your position is under pressure, you can sacrifice some material (a pawn or even a piece) to get the upper hand again and start a new initiative because the position structure changes after such sacrifice. Giving back material is a very usual trick to get out of a sticky situation, especially if you are ahead in material you can still lose some material and gain initiative instead. It is the initiative which is important, material is of secondary importance. Don't be afraid to sacrifice, if it yields a superior position.

"Fischer was a master of clarity and a king of artful positioning. His opponents would see where he was going, but were powerless to stop him."

— *Garry Kasparov*

In each move you need to assess your position vs your opponent and know for sure the balance at any given time (are you materially ahead or behind? What about positionally? Are there any checkmating threats for any of the sides? What are the options for both sides?) and plan ahead. These are done in the form of calculations in different lines. Each line has a sequence of moves and can lead to a certain position. The final position of each line needs to be calculated and assessed correctly. Decision making should only be made on the objective evaluation for the final position of each line. The side that can see, calculate and evaluate more moves ahead and know the tricks and threats along the way is going to be more powerful and successful.

LIFE PRINCIPLE #2

The Situation and each side's threats prevail over the material difference. If a side has the initiative to create a threat, they usually can take advantage of the opportunity and overcome the material disadvantage, if they can find the correct continuation. In real life they say: Location, Location, Location!

LIFE PRINCIPLE #3

Calculate every step precisely, predict the outcome of each step and evaluate different outcomes and choose the most powerful decision. Going with the 2nd best is also good, not as good as finding the most precise move (best move), but if you can't, don't waste a lot of time on any given move and try to make sound moves quickly.

Each move needs to be calculated and be the most powerful in the sense to give you more control, more space, material advantage or a certain type of positional advantage that can eventually yield results and change the balance in your favor. You should be able to justify each move, using the rules in this book. Why did you make it, was it for an attack, defense, or something else? Was it a decoy? What is the longer term plan and how does this move fit into that plan?

White has a slight advantage from the start because it's white to start the game and white is up a tempo. Statistically white wins more because of the extra tempo, but black can equalize (even in the opening) if played solidly.

LIFE PRINCIPLE #4

Give yourself time on critical situations and decisions. Calculate each combination of moves and try to think many moves ahead.

If you have an advantage (of any form: positional, material, space) it's best to try to increase the same type of advantage in the next moves.

LIFE PRINCIPLE #5

One side may have a slight advantage at the start, but that doesn't mean it will remain like that.

LIFE PRINCIPLE #6

Work on your strengths and make the same advantages more prominent.

> *"He Who knows when he can fight and*
> *when he cannot will be victorious."*
>
> — *Sun Tzu*

When you're down materially or your position is inferior, it will become harder to attack. If you're down in material, you have no right to attack, unless you have a clear plan of attack (sequence of moves) that will result in a position that is in your favor. You must only attack when your position allows you to do so.

You must choose your fights very wisely and do not engage in every fight. Especially the ones which are offered to you by the opponent (to engage, take or exchange) are dangerous.

If it's best for your opponent to play on the king side, try to not play on that side, but play in the center or queen side. Don't play in their ground, instead play your own plan. Play on the side that benefits you, not your opponent.

You must know the overall situation and only attack when it's time to attack. On the other hand, defend if it's time to defend. Develop and improve your position by playing strong moves, if it's time to save time and play ok moves.

LIFE PRINCIPLE #7

Only be aggressive when your position allows and you have the right to. If you're behind in position or have been pushed back, you have to be extra careful with attacks. It can overextend you very quickly, if you're not careful. On the other hand if it's a calculated line and you know it yields results, you can be aggressive.

When down materially you have to be extra careful with your king's safety while devising a plan to change the balance in your favor. Play solidly even if you're down materially. The chances will show themselves to equalize or even get ahead.

This is one of the cornerstones of the winning mentality to never let go regardless of the balance of power. Whether you're behind or ahead, always look for weaknesses in the position. If you can't find a weakness in your opponent's position, encourage them to make a weakening move or find a resource that you can use to create a diversion, a counter-attack of another type. Always have something up your sleeve and calculate all critical lines ahead and be ready for all of them.

LIFE PRINCIPLE #8

When on the back foot, you have to think of defenses first. Think of how to not to get pushed back further, before planning an attack. Think of establishing and solidifying your current position.

Each exchange has to be closely calculated and evaluated. No exchange should get initiated by us if it doesn't yield a clear advantage. However, sometimes we may initiate an exchange because the alternative is worse and if we don't, the end position will be far worse for us. This is when we are forced to exchange. It's not good to be forced, so your position is worse, but still accepting the exchange saves you from a worse alternative.

If we have the option to enter the end-game (by initiating exchanges), we should only do so if the resulting end-game will be in our favor. If things are not in our favor or unclear, wait until the time is right. Never initiate an exchange unless your calculations show it's going to result in a clear advantage for you.

LIFE PRINCIPLE #9

No meeting, interaction, email, discussion (formal or informal) have to be initiated by you unless you're sure it yields a positive result in your favor. If you're offered an exchange, only engage if it benefits you, otherwise carry on with your plan and ignore their exchange offer.

If you think you've found a good move, look for a better one. You can't take the first good move (no matter how good the move is) and not study the other options. If you're able to checkmate in 1, taking material doesn't make sense. Always make the strongest move which comes with the most attack or if you're defending choose the best defensive measures. There is almost always a way to explain and justify the best move: Moving pieces forward, creating a pin, adding pressure, controlling the center, creating threat, controlling an important file with a rook, controlling an important diagonal with a bishop, removing the defender, attracting the king to a non-optimal square with a sacrifice, destroying the center, opening up the position because their king is stuck in the middle. There's almost always an explanation for the best / strongest move. If you don't see the justification yet, you need to look better. It's on you to find it. It's there. If you think enough you see the best move. You have to learn and think about that best move and try to learn the patterns for future games.

LIFE PRINCIPLE #10

Never be greedy and take the obvious moves which may be in your favor (and very sweet) but you may lose a better move. In every situation, you're expected to choose the BEST move which results in the most advantageous situation.

Calculate each move very precisely and individually. Every move changes the dynamic of the position and creates some gaps and weaknesses. All threats and tricks by your opponent need to be calculated and evaluated on each move. Check for blunders and mistakes on each move. Sometimes a plan (which might be correct at the time) is still in your head, but with the change of moves that plan may not be valid anymore (but in your head it still is!). These wrong or changed plans that you may act on, but there's a miscalculation somewhere or it was valid before but not anymore, can hurt a lot. Always recalculate and re-imagine the end position, if possible several times. Committing moves can be hard to undo.

LIFE PRINCIPLE #11

Reason and calculate.

Knowing usual tactics is extremely important: Pin, Skewer, Fork, Discovery checks, double checks, windmill. Both absolute and relative pins are specifically important because they limit the piece activity and are considered forcing.

LIFE PRINCIPLE #12

You need to be aware of the usual
tricks that people play on you.

Knowing Zugzwang positions is extremely important. Limiting your opponent's moves to a point where any move that they make is bad for them, is the way to go.

LIFE PRINCIPLE #13

Put your opponent in a position that every action they take is shooting themselves in the foot.

Know the value of pieces (Q>R>B>N>P) and consider the values when exchanging. You normally don't want to exchange a piece for an inferior piece, unless the sacrifice can be justified by a better end position.

Good chess positions are hard to build, it's always a grind. Advantages and disadvantages of both sides in the opening should be very little, if the opening is played well by both sides.

Be a solid, strong player that always comes up ahead by out-thinking their opponent. This could be in the form of better time management, finding weaknesses in their opponent's position and attacking those weaknesses, playing solidly, playing confusingly, setting up traps, tricking your opponent or any other way. The way you do it, doesn't really matter. As long as you're using legal moves on the board to come up with a superior position, you will be the winner.

Consider every possible move (regardless of whether it makes sense or not) and calculate precisely and evaluate. Even crazy moves like queen sacrifice or sacrifices made on empty squares must be considered and calculated. There could be a combination that will yield a decisive advantage. Sometimes sacrificing a piece on an empty square can have great effects.

After a good sacrifice don't be materialistic, be opportunistic. It doesn't matter if they are 2 queens ahead, if you checkmate opponent's king earlier.

In opening you are mostly utilizing your half of the board to develop pieces. An attack, or an indication that an attack might be close is when you commit to push pawns from your side (your half) into enemy territory. If you have more control on one side of the board (right, center or left hand), that's also an indication that you're going to attack on that side. The direction of the pawn chain is also showing that you're going to eventually attack on that side.

Know the weakness and power of each piece Bishops are good in an open game or in an end-game with play on both sides of the board. Knights on the other hand are particularly good in closed positions where central pawns are locked into position. Know the pieces and their real value (in that particular position) and trade your bad pieces for your opponent's best pieces. For example if you have a bad bishop and your opponent has a monster knight placed in an outpost that can not be harassed by your pawns, you can happily trade your bad piece for opponent's good piece. On the other hand, if your opponent offers you an exchange of their bad piece with your good piece, try to avoid the exchange if you can.

You don't have to be perfect and always find the best moves all the time, nobody can do this, not even masters. Computers have been playing better than chess grand masters for decades. You just have to be better than your opponent, have less mistakes than your opponent and play more accurately than them.

If your opponent sacrifices a piece, it's on you to calculate the lines to refute it.

"A sacrifice is best refuted by accepting it."

— *Wilhelm Steinitz*

Sacrifices must be calculated based on the compensation you get out of them. If the compensation is meaningful and the end position is superior, it's a sound sacrifice and must be made. Don't hesitate to shed some material to gain a superior position.

Keep enough time and brain power for the endgame while not blundering in the opening and middle game. This is why it's so important to be able to make ok moves all the time, especially in opening and middle game; to preserve time and brain power for later in the game where the complexity of the position demands it.

A big part of visualization is thinking in what-if scenarios. What if that bishop wasn't there? Then I'd have a great threat. Let's think about a way to remove the bishop and execute the plan, if it's still valid.

Very strong players have super strong imaginations when it comes to positions. They even consider illegal moves! Why? Because pieces move around and it might become possible to create those imaginative positions, by shuffling some pieces in a couple of moves. The end position may not be exactly what you imagined (your opponent has a say in the game too) but the end position is always similar to what you imagined. You are familiar with the motif because you calculated a similar line in your head. Very strong players have very strong imaginations.

Knights are extremely powerful in forking pieces, especially rooks. Knight's special L move is unique between pieces and it's the only chess piece that can jump over other pieces. The disadvantage of a knight is it's slow. In the case of an end game where there's pawns on both sides of the board a bishop is better over a knight because of maneuver speed and range.

Bishops are archers; Many times it's best to keep them tucked back supporting other pieces from far.

There are situations where a knight may be preferred to a bishop. Knights are better in closed games (with lots of pawns). A bishop which is restricted in movement by pawns or doesn't have an open diagonal to operate is not a good bishop. If you have a bad bishop which is entrapped by your own pawns, always try to trade it for a good piece of your opponent.

Fianchetto bishops are extremely powerful when there are no pawns in the center blocking them.

The idea is to not make a move unless you're able to justify it correctly based on calculation, evaluation and decision (which means it's a good move). If you can't find the best move, assign as much time as possible to it. However, you should not waste 1 second of your time. If you know the best move, play it and save time.

Many games, especially on lower levels, soon end in a quick blunder or mistake by one side which gives enough chances to the other side to win the game. In professional and higher level games however, both sides play accurately most of the time and it's about which side plays less accurately and makes a mistake sooner. An accurate line is the shortest amount of moves to checkmate or to get into a position with clear advantage. In the end game there may be several checkmates, but players must play the most accurate moves. There's almost always a most accurate move and then 2nd best, 3rd best and so on. In the middle of the list of possible moves are a bunch of ok moves and then a long list of suicidal play.

One should try to find the best and most accurate move or the closest to it. Both time and brain power are rare resources and should be used very wisely. Tiring your mind over meaningless calculations, especially early in the game, when you know the best move or "sound looking developing moves" is bad. You have to preserve your brain's calculation power as much as possible. In grandmaster games you can see that they play the opening by the book (both sides are good at opening, know the lines and best responses to tricks in that line). In the middle game they play quickly but may think for a minute or two. They take their time right after they are out of the book and analyze the situation. If they feel it's a critical position they may even think very deeply about the position. and analyse the possibilities for both sides. Plan ahead for the next couple of moves to gain a clear advantage.

In any given position, if they think it's critical (meaning there's chances for one side to change the equation drastically if they can find the best move/line) they analyze more and get deeper into possible lines, evaluate them each and choose the one which gives them the best chances of getting ahead or remaining in the game in an equal position. Being able to quickly find an ok move which keeps the position equal is super important.

At any given time, there's a number of legal moves that we can choose from. If our position is:

- **Very good:** majority of moves ahead will result in a better position or even checkmate.

- **Good:** Most of the legal moves will keep the advantage. There still could be suicidal (bad moves) to be aware of. It's important to push forward and increase the advantage.

- **Average:** Some moves ahead will keep the advantage, some will be neutral and some will be bad (losing the advantage or even blundering into a disadvantage)

- **Poor:** Most of the moves ahead will result in a disadvantageous position for us.

- **Very bad:** Most moves are bad, there could be only one move that saves the position and equalizes.

- **Zugzwang** is a position where every move ahead will result in a worse position for the side that is in zugzwang and has to move.

Based on the accuracy of our moves, the number of good or bad options ahead of us changes. If we play accurately, the number of moves ahead that result in a better position will increase. If we play inaccurate moves, the number of good moves reduces and many moves ahead will become bad for us.

You also can interpret this the other way: If many of the moves ahead are good for us (we're spoiled for choice) it means our position is superior, we've played good and accurate moves or the opponent has played badly. In such situations the game is more forgiving for us. While we should do our best to always find the most accurate move, if we can't find it and play 2nd or 3rd best move, still the game will continue with us being ahead.

If we're struggling to find a good move ahead and most moves seem to result in a worst position for us, it means we're under pressure and our position is inferior. In this situations the game is less forgiving and more mistakes can result in a quick loss. We have to be more careful, analyse better and spend more time to find accurate moves that gets us back into the game, either by a counter attack or defending properly and building a better position from there.

LIFE PRINCIPLE #14

In life (unlike chess) you're not forced to make a move. You can do nothing, but doing nothing is also a move.

It's important to analyse all the possible and legal moves ahead and choose the one that gives us the best chances of getting into an advantageous position.

However the general rule is the same between life and chess: When your position is better, more moves will result in your favor. If your position is inferior, more moves could be blunders/mistakes and the number of good moves (that result in an incremental improvement in your position) reduces because you are under pressure.

An abundance of good moves is a sign of a healthy and superior position. On the other hand, if your options are limited and most moves ahead (or all of them) result in a worse position for you, it's a sign of a weak position.

What you allow to happen is also part of your moves. You have the ability to restrict opponents' moves, if you don't use your chances to do so and allow them free development or easlity creating threats, that's also your problem. What you allow is as important is to what you do.

Don't make a move until you're sure (or semi-sure given the time constraint) it's the best move. You are supposed to find the best or closest to best move, on each move. It's better to lose on time rather than moving quickly based on emotions or haunches. You have to see the lines before making the move. You have to have a plan (even a vague one) rather than playing aimlessly. A bad plan is always better than not having one.

LIFE PRINCIPLE #15

Don't get emotional if your opponent seems to know the line and plays very quickly. It's possible that they are tricking you.

They may look very confident, but in real life it's more likely that a quick move that they've just made as a reflex might be a mistake.

7 imbalances in chess are: 1-initiative, 2-material, 3-pawn structure, 4-minor pieces (superior/inferior), 5-development, 6-space and 7-weak squares. Two aspects are more important than the rest: Initiative and material. Initiative is the ability to force the tempo of the moves.

If you calculated a line to have a clear advantage for you, always choose that line over a vague checkmate. A definite advantage is always better than an interesting line which might result in a checkmate, but we can't calculate it in full. Don't exchange pieces when you control more space.

Do as much damage with a piece which you are losing. This sometimes leads to an advantage.

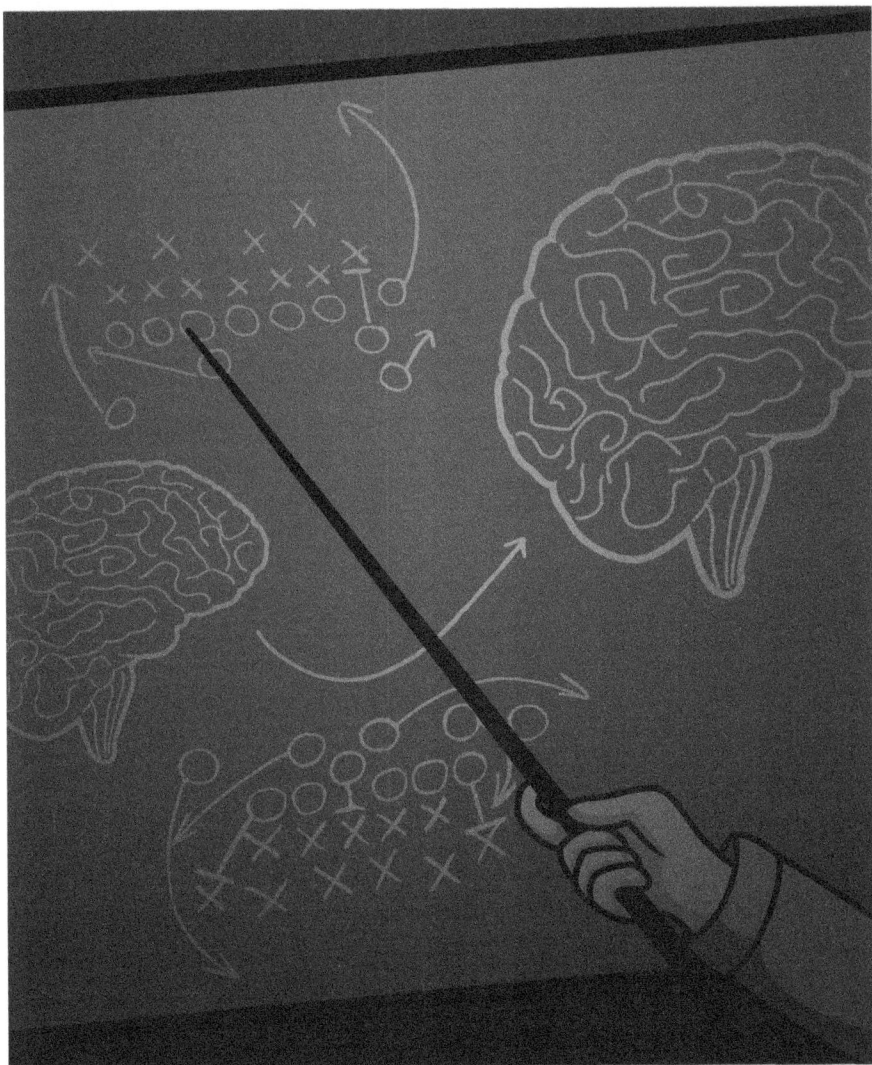

CHAPTER 2

STRATEGIC USE OF RESOURCES

CHAPTER 2
STRATEGIC USE OF RESOURCES

Manage time properly. Use minimum time for opening, enough time for middle game and keep plenty of time for end-game.

You don't have to be perfect and always find the best moves all the time, nobody can do this, not even masters. Computers have been playing better than chess grand masters for decades. You just have to be better than your opponent, have less mistakes than your opponent and play more accurately than them.

Masters move instantly and it turns out to be correct most of the time, that's because they know the patterns and usual tactics. When they see a position instead of instantly calculating all the lines, they try to rely on their visual memory of similar patterns they have encountered or studied in the past. They calculate all the meaningful lines, for themselves and the opponent. It's very important to know which part of the board to focus on because the calculation power of the human brain (and even computers) is limited. Nobody can calculate every line and it's not required either. You have to know where to focus your attention. Where is the current battlefield? What are the threats for both sides?

The importance of time management also comes from the fact that brain power is limited. We get tired or mix up lines after several lines of calculations. It's not easy to visualize pieces moving. Exchanges are harder to visualize because it's not easy to imagine a piece being removed from the board when it is still on the board. Several consecutive captures on the same square is also hard to calculate, but it's a must to visualize and master.

You should know or guess which position is the critical move of the game and spend enough brain power on it. This is why the opening is played very quickly and based on known book moves. To spend less time and brain power until later in the game where the position becomes more complex and needs more calculations. The end-game is particularly important and brain intensive, because the possibilities of tricks increase the later it is in the game. When pieces get traded down, the position opens up and possibilities increase for both sides. Possibilities are threats or tricks by both sides.

Keep enough time and brain power for the endgame while not blundering in the opening and middle game. This is why it's so important to be able to make ok moves all the time, especially in opening and middle game; to preserve time and brain power for later in the game where the complexity of the position demands it.

The way a person assigns time to each move has a great effect on their play and results. This might be the most deciding factor in a game as both sides use the same logic and brain power to analyse the situation, but the side that doesn't waste time on the moves that they know and save their energy for when they're going to need it, will eventually win. Finding the critical move (s) of the game and spending enough time on analyzing the position and finding threats for both sides is of utmost importance.

Winners are not the ones with better calculation speeds, but they also have perfected the decision making on time assigned to each move with the criticality level of the position. Knowing when is the time to find an ok move and when is the time to pressure your mind to analyze the position deeply (and spending your valuable calculation juice), is a skill that you have to perfect.

This is why openings are played very quickly by both sides (based on standard book moves), the middle game is played relatively fast while keeping an eye on not making mistakes. Keep most of your time and brain power for the end-game where the situation gets more complicated and the cost of mistakes gets higher. A mistake or inaccuracy in the end-game most likely will result in a loss for whichever side that makes the mistake.

The amount of pressure you can put on your mind to analyse the position is limited, this is why the side that can keep more of their time and brain resource for later in the game, usually wins.

A grandmaster plays very quickly at the start, thinks and decides fast in the middle game (unless it's a critical move that can affect the result dramatically). In the complex positions arising in the end game they use most of their energy to analyze to either prove their opponent's move wrong or play accurately themselves to push the opponent back and win the game.

Strong players save their valuable time throughout the game and assign most of their time to the critical positions of the game. Critical position is where your move can create a big difference in the result (e.g. Gaining clear advantage, equalizing an otherwise lost position or finding the only move to get you out of a worse position).

It's very important to note that critical position mostly happens during the middle game; sometimes in the end-game and rarely in the opening. If your opponent plays a normal and known opening (which is recommended for both sides) the chances of a critical position in the opening is very slim. This is why openings are played very quickly for both sides based on known book moves. If the opponent plays unorthodox moves in the opening (diverging from book) it's likely that there might be chances to gain advantage and you might want to spend the time and exploit the weak move. However, don't waste too much time in the opening, otherwise you'll get in time trouble in the end-game.

Middle game is where most of your time will be normally spent because it's full of possibilities and weaknesses that show themselves for both sides.

Also in the end-game chances of a critical position is high because of an open board due to exchanges; The open board increases the options for both sides.

It's very important to always predict your opponent's best moves (from their perspective). You must know what's their strongest move and when they actually play the move, if they have found the strongest move (for them) you have already calculated it and know the continuation. However, if they don't play the move you considered to be the strongest for them, it must raise your suspicion and surprise. You need to analyze their actual move (in comparison to what you considered to be their strongest move). If you've made a mistake in predicting their best move (and the move they actually played is stronger than what you predicted) then you must revise your previous calculations and adjust the plans accordingly. However, if their move is weaker than what is best for them, it's a sign that it might be a critical position, because chances are their move is inferior and can be punished. This is why you assign more time to these moves. Whenever your opponent makes a mistake or inaccurate move, it's a sign of a critical position and you must assign more time to exploit that weakness to the maximum possible.

Remember if your opponent makes a BMI   (blunder/mistake/inaccuracy) but you fail to detect or exploit it on time, it's like your position took a hit. Unpunished mistakes of your opponent are your worst enemy. Remember that mistakes and inaccuracies are unavoidable for humans and they are bound to happen (for both sides), it is your duty to predict and find these opportunities, fully analyze them and punish them to the maximum.

Strong players develop an intuition for predicting strong moves of their opponent, so when they are faced with a weak move they get surprised and then try to analyze the opportunity to convert that mistake into a clear advantage for themselves.

Never allow the speed of your opponent to decide how much time you spend on each move (don't allow your opponent to coerce you into moving quickly). The amount of time and brain power spent on each move should be solely based on the criticality of the position and the objective expected result from calculating lines. Don't let emotions interfere with resource allocation.

Humans have a tendency to play faster when the opponent plays faster or slower when the opponent takes their time. It's super important to reduce the emotional effects that your opponent's style of play may have on your decision making. Your moves should always be calculated correctly and accurately. The selection of the move should be solely based on the evaluation of the position.

The opposite is also sometimes true: When the opponent makes a very quick reflexive move, it's more likely to be a bad move. It's a good practice to take your time and analyse the position more deeply, right after the opponent has made a hasty move without thinking enough about it. If you get emotional and also make a quick hasty move, you've lost your chance to find the weakness in their move.

Mind of a chess player is torn between the decision to act on the move they consider best based on their calculations so far (i.e., not wasting any more time, saving time for later) and the decision to take more time now to calculate because they think the current position might be critical and worth the investment of time and brain power to calculate.

Everybody's brain has limited capacity in calculation of chess lines, this is proven because computers play better than the best human grandmasters for decades now and humans gets tired after calculations. It's a balancing act between assigning enough time to each move (to make strong moves and not make blunders) and at the same time trying to use the least amount of time (while calculating as quickly as possible) to save time for later, which makes a great chess player.

Yes, the person with better tactical awareness has an advantage, but if you choose the wrong move to invest valuable time in, you may not have enough time to think when the critical position comes. What's more important is the critical position of the game where there's a short window of opportunity for one side to get ahead and whether they find and exploit it or not.

You need time to convert a winning end-game, save the time for later in the game, as much as possible. However this shouldn't come at the cost of making mistakes or blunders early on. You need to make the best possible move with the least amount of time.

Also keep in mind that opening is more forgiving in terms of mistakes than end-game. A mistake in the end-game will more likely result in you losing the game than a mistake in the opening. This is because the game becomes less forgiving later in the game. This is basically why we need to save time for later in the game.

Every human has limited brain power to calculate lines, this ability gets better by practice but nonetheless it's a limited resource and should be used wisely and invested very carefully in each move.

Also, humans have regular blindspots in chess: For some reason many humans have difficulty visualizing the pieces moving back.

The blunders/mistakes of humans have embarrassing similarities. Even grandmasters make the same mistakes, this has to do with the way our mind is wired or maybe the way we are taught chess that causes us to be blind to certain positions.

It is normal for your brain to not be able to continue the calculation of a certain line, everybody stops at some point. Some positions are harder to visualize for humans.

However, it is super important to force your mind to only end the calculation only when it's your opponent's turn to move, not your turn. If you can't visualize the line anymore and decide to stop, rebuild it in your mind again and force your mind to go at least one step forward in calculation until it's your opponent's turn to move, not yours. If your mind is tired or you don't have the time to calculate or you just can't visualize the position anymore, push yourself to recalculate that line up to a point where it's your opponent's turn.

This habit proves to be critical for humans to find weaknesses in the position and analyze the position better for both sides.

Never end the calculation when it's your turn to move. Push at least one step further.

LIFE PRINCIPLE #16

When calculating and analyzing the sequence of actions with the other side, try to always finish the calculations with the strongest action of the other side and not yours.

A chess piece is a resource you have, and each one has its own strengths and weaknesses. You and your opponent are given the same amount of material at the start of the game and the only thing causing imbalance between white and black is the fact that white is up a tempo because of opening the game.

You have to develop your army into meaningful squares as soon as possible and create a solid position while on each move trying to avoid tactical mistakes.

Most human games are lost because one side doesn't detect and exploit the other side's mistake/inaccuracy on time. Tactical opportunities appear for both sides throughout the game, but it's your duty to reduce your vulnerability in terms of tactics and at the same time find tactical opportunities in your opponent's camp to exploit and get ahead. If you can conduct an attack on the opponent's king, you must do it. Otherwise you can choose to play a sound grinding game and try to win small advantages (being up a piece or up the exchange or having more space or control over center) and build on that same advantage to make it a clear decisive advantage that you can convert into a won game.

CHAPTER 3

EXPLOITING YOUR OPPONENTS' MISTAKES

CHAPTER 3
EXPLOITING YOUR OPPONENTS' MISTAKES

Pay attention to the "Style of play" of your opponent. Your job (apart from making sound judgements and good moves on the board) is to detect when they blunder or make mistakes (and they do), use it wisely and on time. Punishment of bad moves should be done in the harshest and strongest possible way, immediately. If you are not always monitoring your opponent's mistakes, you're wasting a lot of good information. You can't just focus on your own moves. Many of your moves are responses to their move, either to defend if they create a threat or push forward when they make mistakes or get complacent.

Each player has a specific style of play. Everybody has blindspots and it is your job to find and exploit those mistakes, right when they happen.

It is very important to severely punish mistakes immediately. If you lose tempos, they might be able to escape from a bad position and defend properly, let's say they have a piece hanging, but you don't take it. They move it on the next move and defend it. If they do, it gets harder for you to push forward because you lost a chance to get ahead. Losing a chance to punish your opponent's mistake is as bad as losing your own pieces. If this happens there's always some sort of concession coming from it too and you'll eventually be punished for not taking the chance. Response must be immediate and be the most powerful. Immediate here doesn't mean to move hastily, but to punish on the very next move and don't allow them to escape from a bad position. The window of opportunity to punish a bad move closes quickly, if you don't exploit it on time. Find the usual blindspots of your opponent and try to predict or provoke them. It's good to calculate all the lines (which makes sense or doesn't) for your opponent too and know that a specific move is bad for them. But it's easy to miscalculate for them, because of blindspots of humans in general or weakness of this specific player. If they play that bad move, you can comfortably follow your calculated plan and end up in a superior position. This is a style of play by itself (playing solid and defensive). There's many styles of play and you need to be ready for them. Some people just use time more wisely and always get ahead because of it, they are able to put their opponent in time pressure.

Playing mysteriously and tricking your opponent is also another effective style of play. You must learn most styles of play and be comfortable to respond to all in a cold, calculated manner that always puts you in a better position.

If your opponent makes a move that you didn't expect, take enough time to study the position even more deeply; if you didn't expect it (as part of good candidate moves for them) it's probable that it might be a mistake. When calculating lines, you ought to find and calculate the best moves for your opponent too. You normally expect them to play the best move in the position for themselves, but if they can't and play another move instead, it's likely it's subpar for them. This is the best time to punish those bad moves.

Playing solidly and defensively is also a style of play, however you need very deep knowledge to play defensively and wait for your opponent to make mistakes to exploit them. It is recommended to not play defensively unless you are a master who knows what they are doing. Playing defensively can lead into gridlock positions where it's only your opponent who can push for an advantage, this is a bad position to be in. With playing defensively you are intentionally developing your army a little behind (compared to a balanced game) and looking for your opponent to over-stretch a pawn or piece and then targeting that piece.

It is recommended to adopt an aggressive mindset rather than defensive, however you can play defensively if you've mastered aggressive play.

Looking at grandmasters analysing the time it takes them to solve puzzles it's clear that humans have common blindspots: it takes grandmasters longer to solve harder puzzles, their mind and yours work the same and suffer from the same blindspots. Note that for a computer this has no effect as computers don't have blindspots and emotions and analyse positions objectively, but humans have common blindspots and suffer from emotions. For some reason humans have issues visualizing certain positions. It's still unclear what makes a position harder for a human mind to analyse, however what's important is to take note of this phenomenon. This book is designed to help you win more games against humans.

If a move is good for your opponent, never force them to make that move. Instead force or encourage them to make mistakes (other moves than the best move for them) and even provoke those mistakes. Use decoys, tricks (a fake attack for example) or other tactics to stop them from making the best move for themselves.

If your opponent stops your plan by playing a move that seemingly shuts down your intent, still check the plan. Many times their move is just weakening their position further and making your plan more effective.

"Play the opening like a book, the middle game like a magician, and the endgame like a machine."

— *Spielmann*

It's super important to keep enough of your fighting spirit and time for the end game. Chess is all about the end-game, opening is meant to be fast and reliable. Middle game is supposed to be solid, mysterious and cunning. End-game is where games are won or lost. The number of chances and possibilities increase over time and in the end-game there's almost always tricks to be played for both sides because the board gets empty and open and scope and mobility of pieces increase. If you want to learn Chess properly, you need to master the end-game first. Converting a won game is a must have skill and you should never let a lost opponent flee from their bad position. Don't give chances, instead increase the pressure.

By adding pressure to the position you can put the opponent in a position where they are forced into an unfavorable position. If you can put your opponent where they are forced to make a specific move, because the alternative is worse for them, you are in the superior position. This is the ultimate sign. Sometimes you can create a checkmate threat and force the opponent to sacrifice an important piece to stop the checkmate. That's the way to play the game. You should always be the one delivering the punches or if not, add to the pressure and create long term plans and threats. Threats of a checkmate (or even hinting it) is super effective because it almost always comes with a concession on your opponent's part because they have to respond/mitigate that threat and this gives you time to orchestrate the plan even further and pressure the position even more. Increase the pressure to push to victory.

You should learn end-games and usual checkmate patterns before studying openings. It is expected of you to convert a won game without giving concessions of any sort. If your opponent goes back, you go forward. If they play a weakening move, you must analyze, plan and exploit it with the strongest move. Analyze which squares will be weak/soft after that weakening move? Many weakening moves are pawn moves in front of their king. A protected king has pawns in front of him and if someone is forced to move pawns in front of their king, it's a sign of weakness and we should study the position to see what squares will become weak and how to exploit that weakness?

On every move the priorities are: First to not make a blunder. That's why you should always blunder-check your move right before making the move. Check the sequence in your mind again, are your calculations correct?

Check for inaccuracies: Ask yourself, "How this move can be bad?" Try to prove yourself wrong by calculating again.

Remember, it's ideal to find the best move, but it's much more important to not make blunders, mistakes and inaccuracies.

Making an ok move (which is not a blunder or mistake) is a very important skill to have. You're not expected to always find the best move (even grandmasters make inaccuracies), but it is expected to make very rare blunders and only occasionally make mistakes. In professional games, where both sides are of high caliber (meaning they make very few mistakes), it's always the side that makes the first mistake who pays for it and loses. It's very important to give less concessions and inaccuracies and be ahead of your opponent. The side that makes the first mistake, almost always loses.

A very effective way of play is to find flaws in your opponent's plan. Most of the time it's not you who makes good moves that results in your position to get better, but it's your opponent who makes mistakes and it is your duty to detect it as early as possible, understand why it's a bad plan or a mistake and act upon it. There is no excuse in not detecting your opponent's inaccuracies. You can't just focus on your own moves, but need to analyse your opponent's position as well as you do yours.

On every move you should have candidate best moves for your opponent and if they choose to make another move (i.e. Their move surprises you) you need to analyse more deeply and decide whether your previous assessment (about their best candidate moves) were wrong or maybe their move is truly inferior hence must be punished. If you think of their move to be inferior, you must analyse deeper to find the inaccuracy and exploit/punish it in the best possible manner.

The later it is in the game the more impactful moves become. A mistake in the opening has less impact than a mistake in the end game. In an end game it is more critical to play the most accurate move. Opening is more forgiving than the middle game and the middle game is more forgiving than the end game. This is why most of the time and brain power must be kept for the end game, where the importance of calculation becomes tenfold. A mistake in the opening could be overcome by playing solid moves after it, but a mistake in the end game is more likely to decide the loser.

When thinking in terms of vulnerability of opponent's position and pieces, think of the way each piece is weak:

- **Rooks** are weak from the diagonal side because they only move straight. Rooks can be pinned using bishops or queens exploiting their diagonal weakness.

- **Bishops** are weak from horizontal/vertical side because they only move diagonally. Rooks can hunt down bishops easily.

- **Knights** and bishops can be pressured, pushed around and hunted down using pawns. Pawn moves that dislodge a knight from an important square are usually very strong.

- **Knights** are usually slower than bishops. In an end-game with opportunities on both sides of the board bishops are better (in attack and defense) because of their range and speed.

If your opponent doesn't play aggressively and gives you easy access to take control of the center or infiltrate or any other type of advantage, it is your duty to take the opportunity and get ahead. You mustn't play defensively when your opponent plays defensively. If they offer you an easy win or advantage, always take it and put even more pressure on their position. There's no excuse in not taking an opportunity when presented to you, unless you have reason to believe it's a trap and it's best not to engage.

If the opponent plays a bad move (instead of a good move), you need to analyse it in your head and know for sure the evaluation of that move. If it is truly a bad move, they've done serious damage to their position and there must be a way for you to take advantage of it and punish that bad move to the maximum possible. If you play the best move in response to a bad move, your position improves drastically and the chances of you winning increases.

LIFE PRINCIPLE #17

If the opponent makes an obvious mistake, never get out of character or complacent — respond in the most respectful but strongest manner. The way to refute a bad move is to make normal good moves.

Humans have a tendency to get complacent when the opponent gives them room to be complacent. It's super important to not get complacent or get emotional (happy) but to still make calm, calculated, solid decisions and actions.

CHAPTER 4

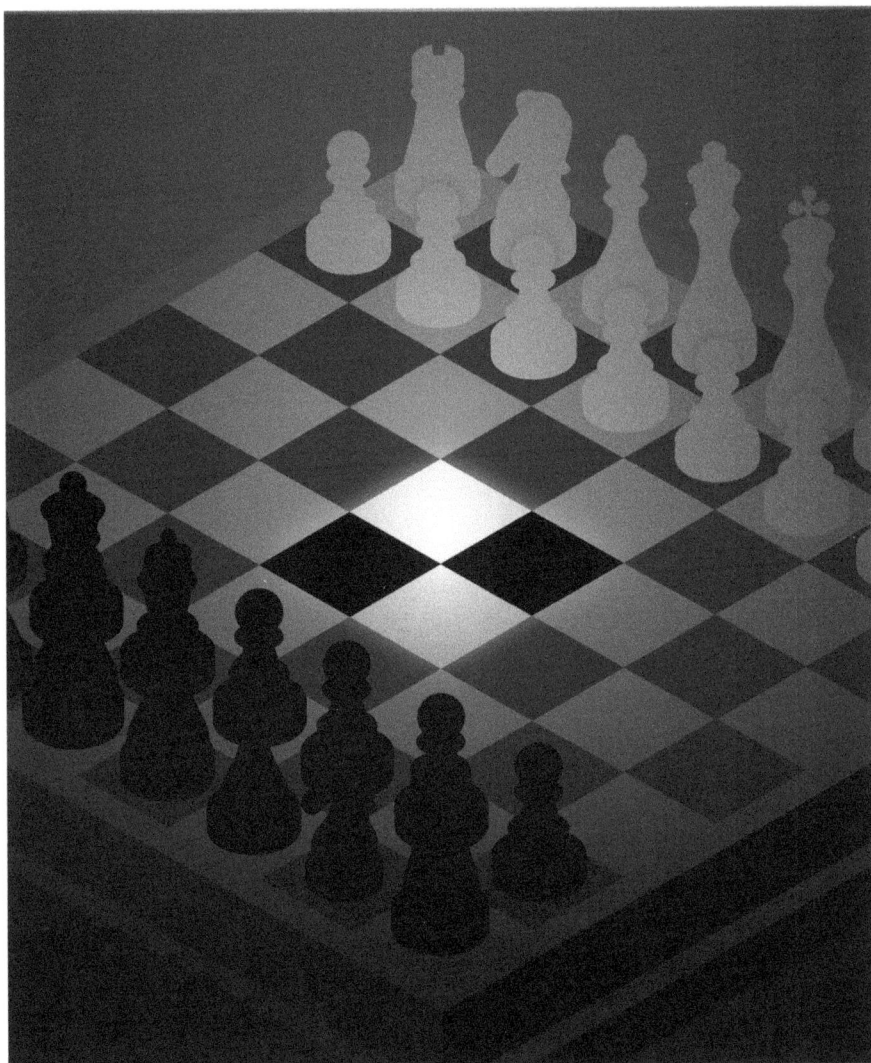

IMPORTANCE OF CENTER

CHAPTER 4
IMPORTANCE OF CENTER

Control the center with your pawns and pieces. The center of the board is where you can exert more control over the rest of the board in all directions. It's like the highest point of a battleground. It's the most strategic part of the board. Try to control the center, occupy the center with your pieces and restrict your opponent from controlling or occupying the central squares.

Never exchange a central pawn of yours for a non-central pawn of your opponent. If they manage to force you to do so, it's a blow to your position.

LIFE PRINCIPLE #18

Be aware of the obvious things and cover all the main aspects.

Central pawns, pieces that occupy the center or control the central squares effectively are very important. Try to gain as much central control as possible and at the same time stop your opponent from gaining control over key central squares.

If you have a pawn in one of the 4 central squares of the board, but your opponent doesn't have anything, it's a sign you've played well. If you control more of the central squares with your pieces, it's a sign your position is superior to your opponent. If you can put a piece in one of the central squares which can not be kicked with a pawn— we call these "outposts"— it's a sign your position is superior. In the endgames centralizing the queen is a very usual maneuver to maximize its influence throughout the board.

"Tactics flow from a superior position."

— Bobby Fischer

Improve and enhance your position as much as possible and tactical opportunities will arise. Especially when you control the center, your pieces have the mobility to move in any direction. This lends itself to lots of tactical opportunities.

Attack happens mostly with pushing the pawns. Try to use your pawns wisely and push them forwards. Pawns that can check squares around the enemy king can be extremely powerful.

The game of chess is easy to win, if you align your moves with the following 3 concepts:

1. Central control   **2.** Development   **3.** King safety

Apart from the above 3 concepts you also need to have tactical awareness. Tactical awareness is the ability to calculate lines and find the best move in any position. To improve your tactical awareness you need to train your mind to solve chess tactics.

- **Central control:** Controlling the central 4 squares of the board with your pieces, either by putting your pieces in the center or exerting pressure and controlling those central squares using your pieces. Devising plans to stop your opponent from taking control of the center is part of the central control strategy.

- **Development:** Developing pieces into meaningful squares to work as a coordinated army together. Also devising plans to stop your opponent from developing their pieces into good squares for them is part of this concept.

- **King safety:** Think about your own king's safety and vulnerabilities as well as the opponent king's safety and weaknesses.

If you can: **1.)** control the center of the board, **2.)** develop your pieces into meaningful squares that can work together as a coordinated army and **3.)** keep your king safe while exploiting the opponent king's weaknesses, you will win the game.

CHAPTER 5

IMPORTANCE OF DEVELOPMENT

CHAPTER 5
IMPORTANCE OF DEVELOPMENT

Develop your pieces to the squares that make sense for their role in the overall plan. Piece coordination leads to better and superior position. Study the relative position of pieces with each other and how they can help each other to amplify each other's effect.

LIFE PRINCIPLE #19

Use tactics to increase the potential of your strengths.

Usually, the side with the initiative has more chances of creating threats. Don't be materialistic. The side with less material, but more threats and initiative, often wins — this is why sacrifices are possible and extremely important.

When sacrifices happen, the balance between material and initiative becomes fragile and the side with less material may have a nice combination to expose and checkmate the opponent's king.

Know in what environment each piece flourishes:

- **Bishops** are better in open games, outside of a pawn chain rather than being blocked by its own pawns;

- **Knights** are better in closed games;

- **Rooks** are more powerful in open or semi-open files.

Try to move each piece to their ideal squares with highest potential and better coordination with other pieces.

Rooks are best to put on open or semi-open files. Lift the rook to further ranks when possible. Infiltrate with the rook when the opportunity arises to the furthest rank possible. The more forward a rook lift goes, the more aggressive it usually is. Rooks are especially useful on 7th rank, limiting the king's movement and mobility. Doubling rooks on the same file or rank or even tripling 2 rooks + queen is extremely effective in adding pressure. Rooks are very usefl in limiting the activity of the opponent's king. Put your rook on 7th rank(if you're white) to limit the black king to back rank. Because of the way rooks move and the human brain works, humans don't see the rooks moving horizontally, very well. We tend to miss this moves.

Battery increases the pressure and effect of pieces. [Rook+Rook], [Rook+Rook+Queen] and [Queen+Bishop] batteries are extremely forceful in the sense that they increase the pressure on the opponent's position or a certain square.

A developed coordinated army triumphs over an undeveloped army. The more advanced the pieces are the more control they exert. Worst type of development is back rank fest where many of your pieces haven't left their initial squares. The more forward your pieces are, the more aggressive and effective they are, most of the time. However, if you push pawns or pieces forward without enough support, they may be over-stretched and become a liability.

Only the side with a fully developed army has the right to attack. If you are behind in development you have no right to attack. On the other hand if you are ahead in development, forget about defensive moves and deliver punches: check, capture, threat.

CHAPTER 6

IMPORTANCE OF
KING SAFETY

CHAPTER 6
IMPORTANCE OF KING SAFETY

A king walk (consecutive checks which draws the king from safety towards the enemy pieces) is a sign of a weak king and can result in checkmate most of the time.

Never allow escape squares for your opponent's king. If they manage to hide their king in a safe place, they will start attacking your king.

King walk is an example of forcing move. When a king is exposed (especially in the middle of the board) it gets easy to target it and even checkmate with little material. Sometimes a combination of 2 minor pieces with help of a pawn can deliver the checkmate. Always think about forcing sequences and calculate them very accurately for as many moves as you can. Evaluate the end position for each major line (that makes the most sense) and choose the most powerful moves that the end position is more in your favor, or at least equalize. Don't go back on any move, unless you absolutely have to. Going back comes with consequences, most of the time.

King safety is of utmost importance. No matter how good your position is, if your king is getting checkmated on the next move, no amount of material advantage can save that game. Try to protect your king with pawns and pieces and have a plan for the possible attacks and threats. Castling adds to king protection most of the time. Unpushed pawns are better in front of a king, pushed pawns create holes and weaknesses on the squares that pawns are not protecting anymore. Each pawn push weakens certain squares and you should be aware of them when pushing pawns, especially the ones in front of your own king.

Your king must be tucked away in a safe place (usually a corner, not in the middle of the board) and protected with pawns in front and minor pieces around it. A king which is exposed and is under the attack of checks is a weak king. In the opening and middle-game kings are meant to be kept back in a safe place. If you have to move your king in the opening and middle-game try to move it backwards, not towards enemy pieces. In the end-game however, king is a very important piece and king activity can play an important role in the end-game.

Castling long (especially against a king which is castled short) is an under-utilized attacking move. Castling in general moves two pieces, king and rook. Long castle immediately brings a rook to a central file which can save an important tempo compared to short castle.

Sacrifices around the enemy king have more venom. Many times a piece (bishop, knight, even rooks or sometimes queen) can be sacrificed around the enemy king for a pawn or two to result in a threatening position for you. When attacking you can afford to lose pieces to reduce the defenders around their king.

Focus on your opponent's king! Instead of thinking to get ahead materially or positionally or anything else, first focus on checkmating the king, exposing the king, weaknesses of the king. If you can exploit or create a weakness near the king or remove the defenders of the king, always try to do that first. The game is about checkmating the opponent's king, not winning material or getting ahead positionally. You may have a superior position, but lose a chance to checkmate. A superior position that can not be converted into a win is of no use. You may have more space and a superior position, but the position could be so that you can't push for a win. You must focus your attention on the king, wherever he is or goes.

LIFE PRINCIPLE #20

Choose your battles wisely. Every battle takes time and energy. It's best to focus on the main objectives and not engage with every fight, interaction or exchange presented to you.

King becomes a very strong piece in the end-game. In the opening and middle game it's best to keep the king tucked away behind pawns in a safe place, but in the end game activate the king and move it towards the center (or wherever the battle is). King can double attack pieces and win one of them or limit the mobility of the opponent's pieces or king. Opposition is a king limiting the other king's possible moves.

CHAPTER 7

KEEPING THE TENSION

CHAPTER 7
KEEPING THE TENSION

The balance of power between white and black is very fragile in all stages of the game. If your opponent makes a mistake or a blunder— and they do most of the time, if you allow enough time— you're expected to detect it very soon (or even provoke a weakness to happen) and then lead him down a path that will yield to a worse position for them and a better position for you. Don't force/encourage them to make a good move for them, try to do the opposite.

LIFE PRINCIPLE #21

Choose your battles wisely. Every battle takes time and energy. It's best to focus on the main objectives and not engage with every fight, interaction or exchange presented to you.

The balance of power can change at any given moment. You may make 40 good moves, but if your move 41 is a big blunder and your opponent can utilize it, you'll lose that game. Each move is important and the later it is in the game, the impact of moves becomes more critical.

"Usually the side who makes the last blunder loses the game. "The winner of the game is the player who makes the next-to-last mistake."

— *Savielly Tartakower*

Always remember that. If you made a blunder, continue as solidly as possible and wait for your opponent to make mistakes. Then is your chance to equalize or even get ahead.

LIFE PRINCIPLE #22

Everything is temporary, a good situation may turn into bad with only one bad mistake. It's important to not give up when you're behind and continue making good decisions and actions. It's likely the situation would change in a way that you can take advantage. Others make mistake too and you just have to wait and detect it when they happen.

Creating tension is good, increasing the tension *(i.e. Adding attackers to a pinned piece)* is good. Releasing the tension without gaining a clear advantage is NOT good.

When there is tension (potential for exchange), try to keep the tension and don't accept it, unless you have to *(e.g. You lose material otherwise)*. The side that accepts the tension usually finds themselves in trouble.

This is why when you're ahead materially, you offer exchanges to your opponent (to simplify the position and win the end-game) and they normally avoid it. If they accept the exchange, it's worse for them. The side that offers exchange (when the time is right) has something to gain from the exchange, this is why accepting an exchange is not normally favorable.

LIFE PRINCIPLE #23

If there's an opportunity for an exchange (like a pending meeting) don't take it unless it provides clear advantage for you. Taking the opportunity sooner than required, will actually result in loss. It's best to keep the tension and only release when the following sequence delivers clear results for you.

Having a fluid/flexible position is of utmost importance, especially when the opponent hasn't committed to a plan yet. Committing moves (on your side) should be calculated precisely and only played if we evaluate it to be a valid plan that will result in progress. Fluid pawns are preferred over fixed pawns. Once pawns are pushed forward, they can't come back and once we place a piece on an important outpost in enemy territory, we usually can't easily call him back for defense. If you're under attack you shouldn't be thinking about attacking yourself, but defending properly and turning the position around. Attack is valid only if you have the means to support it with a proper plan. A blind attack with no support is likely to fail.

Flexibility/fluidity of the position is especially important in defense. When the opponent hasn't committed to an attack yet, you have to be ready and remain flexible to defend wherever required. Placing a minor peace on a square where it can be used for both offense and defense is very powerful. Calculate committing moves very precisely, if a move is somewhat committing (meaning that it changes the position) you have to calculate the sequence more precisely. *(e.g. if you're pushing a pawn and it weakens certain squares)*

CHAPTER 8

DECEPTION

CHAPTER 8
DECEPTION

Decoys, deceptions and tricks are a very important part of this game. Sometimes you intentionally put a piece on prey (or artificially blunder it) to get a clear advantage out of the following sequence. You have to outthink your opponent by thinking more moves ahead.

It's important to know the fragility of the balance in chess and the fact that the balance can change a lot with each move. Each move changes the dynamic of the position and needs to be analyzed separately. It is super important to know that after each move you are expected to forget/ delete all the previous analysis and calculations and start calculating all the possible lines again. Previous ideas and lines may or may not still be valid. New lines (with new opportunities and threats) which weren't possible or valid before may come into play and you need to detect and calculate them. Many mistakes happen because a side executes on a plan that was valid before, but now with the moves actually played on the board, that plan may not be valid any more.

You can't act on a plan from previous calculations, unless you double check the calculation and evaluation on each move again. This is one of the most vulnerable parts of our brain and one of those human mind traits which is not useful in chess. You need to control the urge to act on a plan in your mind (because you calculated it before) but try to recalculate again before making it. If still valid, you can act on it. If that plan doesn't work anymore, you need to detect it early on, stop and think of another plan.

"You must take your opponent into a deep dark forest where 2+2=5, and the path leading out is only wide enough for one."

— *Mikhail Tal*

Try to be mysterious and don't play obvious moves giving away your strategic plans early on. Try to disguise your plans and play quiet moves that later on turn out to be purposeful, precise and deadly. Tricking your opponent into thinking in a certain way is the best way to keep them busy with nonsense while you're planning the next moves and lines. Always be on the lookout to trick them with every possible way, psychologically, body language or just your moves on the board. Nobody cares how you won a game, as long as you used legal moves and came on top in the end.

"Mistrust is the most necessary characteristic of the Chess player."

— *Siegbert Tarrasch*

Always ask questions and don't take anything for granted. Nothing is as it seems and moves may have a lot of side consequences other than their face value. Think of the reason behind moves (for yourself and the opponent) and try to out-think your opponent by thinking more deeply and evaluating end-positions more correctly.

It's important to know that there's only 1 rule which is correct 100% of the time: Checkmate the opponent king. All the other rules have less accuracy.

Sometimes it's possible to win a game by an unsound sacrifice, if the opponent doesn't know how to defend the position properly (even though it might be possible for them to defend).

"A good sacrifice is one that is not necessarily sound but leaves your opponent dazed and confused."

— *Rudolph Spielmann*

The earlier a move is made (with the intention of a long term plan) it's better because its intention is concealed. If you make several consecutive moves with a clear plan in mind, you're giving away your plan too easily. Try to conceal your plans with other moves that seem tricky or misleading to your opponent. Never give out your plan too early in the game.

Most of the time the side that can trick the opponent or somehow surprise their opponent, wins. If you manage to hide your intention (or even better, lead your opponent into thinking they know your plan while you're preparing another plan) and execute only when it's time, you'll get ahead of the opponent. The plans and legal moves are limited for both sides, so it's extra important to hide the attacking plan (will you attack on left, right or center? Will you try to go into an end-game or not?) or even lead the opponent to prepare for a wrong plan where in fact your real plan is to do damage somewhere else. This is the way to get ahead: Surprise your opponent.

If you let your plan out early on and give time to your opponent to diffuse it, it'll be hard to get an advantageous position.

You should look weak, where you're strong. You should look at attacking where your intentions are really to disturb the enemy army, create weaknesses and exploit it. This is why you may send a fake attack signal, where in fact your plans are different. Hide your intentions and win the game.

If you feel your position is deteriorating with no progress and you're giving the opportunity to your opponent to take the initiative, you can make a surprising move which is aggressive to create imbalances in the position. Many times such aggressive moves are played in the center.

CHAPTER 9

PATIENCE

CHAPTER 9
PATIENCE

The best way to learn the game is to learn the end-game first. You have to be able to masterfully convert a winning position into a win if you have a decisive advantage. Then try to convert not so obviously won end-games.

You're expected to win if there's a clear advantage *(e.g. +9 difference in material points, meaning you're a queen ahead)*. Then reduce the advantage to +5 and try to win those positions where you're only 5 points ahead. Then reduce the advantage to 3 (a minor piece ahead) and after that as much as possible to +1 or 0, but try to convert them too. This forces you to play strongly in equalish positions. A master is able to convert a tiny advantage into a win. That tiny advantage could be a pawn ahead (+1 advantage) or even equal material with a tiny space advantage.

LIFE PRINCIPLE #24

The later it is, the more important and impactful your moves become. When it's clear what everyone's plan is, flexibility reduces (as options are limited) and precision needs to increase.

What you do in the end and how you treat others in the end of situations is extremely important. Nobody will remember the middle, but everybody remembers the end.

Pay close attention to forcing lines and in-between moves. Never auto-recapture a piece. Captures and exchanges have a very important effect on the dynamics of the position and the whole game, they leave gaps, weaknesses and opportunities on the board. Captures and exchanges result in pieces disappearing from the board, introducing new opportunities and threats. Always look for what remains on the board (and not what comes off). Pay close attention to capture or exchange moves as they change the position's character drastically, i.e. a square which was protected up to now, becomes soft.

All legal moves, even the craziest moves (including sacrifices) must be analyzed. Sometimes opportunities arise to win an advantage, but you must act on the spot and not delay. Don't just look for obvious sacrifices (that come with captures), sacrifices delivered on empty squares can have a super strong effect, but they are harder to see and detect, because of the way the human mind is wired and especially because of materialistic mentality that no one wants to lose a piece for nothing, but if it yields a favorable result, why not? Look for all the possible sacrifices (captures or non-captures) all the time. Find out if any of the sacrifices can trigger a trick and lead to a superior position for you, or your opponent. If your opponent has such a threat you need to calculate it and be ready for it.

Pieces that are put on prey, but are immune to capture have a super strong effect. You can put your piece on a very effective square and your opponent can technically capture it, but the consequences of that capture would be devastating for them meaning it can not be captured without losing the game or losing serious material. This results in the piece to be immune to capture but still be able to exert pressure on the opponent's position.

To the untrained eye it may look like a mistake, you're putting your piece on prey to be captured for free or by an inferior piece, but if the alternative is worse for your opponent that piece can not be captured. These are very strong moves, most of the time.

Don't cash-in too early. If you have a threat, don't take what's obvious. Instead look for another threat to increase the pressure and gain more advantage.

Good chess positions are hard to build, it's always a grind. Advantages and disadvantages of both sides in the opening should be very little, if the opening is played well by both sides.

Be a solid, strong player that always comes up ahead by out-thinking their opponent. This could be in the form of better time management, finding weaknesses in their opponent's position and attacking those weaknesses, playing solidly, playing confusingly, setting up traps, tricking your opponent or any other way. The way you do it, doesn't really matter. As long as you're using legal moves on the board to come up with a superior position, you will be the winner.

Learn how to play equalish/balanced positions. This is how most of the games will be played. Your opponents know the rules too. They will play near to perfect moves up to the very end. They know how to force a weakness even if you are behind in material. Learn to come up with good/acceptable moves very quickly. Maybe you don't find the best move in the position, but you have to always use time wisely and come up with quality actions, moves and plans. If not the best, find the 2nd or 3rd best. Don't waste time. Be as precise and as lean as possible (never waste 1 second as it can be the difference between loss and win in the end-game). This is the only way to consistently get better. Pushing your mind to make better decisions and also calculate more quickly, more deeply and more precisely is the only way to train your mind to do better next time.

Games are won the hard way. There is no easy way, no rule of thumb to use, all the time. Only calculation matters. The side that can visualize the future positions better (final position after a sequence of moves) and correctly evaluate those lines and make rational decisions in the least amount of time is going to win. There's no way out of calculation. The only way to get better at chess is trying to extract a very tiny advantage from the position, then build on that and make it a bigger advantage and eventually win the game. Or, create a new weakness.

LIFE PRINCIPLE #25

Making a sound decision and moving quickly is a great skill to have. You have to always be able to come up with ok decisions and actions. You may not find the best effective action in any given time, but you should be able to not make a blunder and find a sound action very soon. This reduces your time waste during the equalish positions leaving more time for later when you really need to think and find the best moves.

Studying previous games (between grandmasters) is good, but you should be aware of a trap: They make it look so easy. Their moves are just like your moves. Masters are also forced to only make legal moves. The difference between you and a grandmaster is they have calculated so many lines ahead in their mind and base their decision (of what move to play) on that analysis. You may not analyze that deeply and may not see all the nuances in the position. A grandmaster may see more than 10 moves ahead and calculate all the possible lines, see threats along the and best defenses for your side as well as the opponent. That's how they come up with a move, they see the opponent's threats and best moves as well and consider it in their evaluation. And they can do this consistently all the time. It's not that they are only better tactical players, but they manage time better, manage their emotions better, to not affect their decisions. It takes a lot of practice and discipline to force your emotions about the opponent or the position out and only make moves based on the position's objective evaluation. Masters don't get excited, don't play hastily. A master doesn't have an urge to respond immediately (a very important trait in life and chess), calculate, calculate and calculate correctly. GMs manage their overall play in a way to always have enough time and not get into time pressure.

A master can come up with an acceptable move in any given position in a very short amount of time. They also have the potential to think and analyze a given position for hours before making a move. Looking at the play of a master, not just the game, but seeing their faces, emotions, facial expressions and body language, their confidence over time and studying their mindset and mimicking their behavior is a very good learning tool. You'll eventually find and adopt your style of play —not everybody plays the same— but the main traits that cause a player to be successful remain the same.

"Move in silence; only speak when it's time to say checkmate."

— Lorenzo Senni

"If your opponent offers you a draw, try to work out why he thinks he's worse off."

— Nigel Short

Try to default to not accepting draws unless it's clear to you that getting an advantage from the position is impossible for you.

Always blunder check on the last second before making the move. Are you missing something? Was the plan you had in your mind still valid? Does the move you're about to make hang a piece of yours?

Blunder check means imagining the move your are about to make and calculating the best response of the opponent to it. Because of visualization deficiency by humans, many times you realize a move is a blunder right after making the move. This shows your visualization must be improved.

The method of thinking in the end-game should be very different from the method used in the opening and middle game. In the end game you should build long term plans of how to win or if you are behind how to equalize and get a draw. It's relatively useless to think in terms of a long term plan in the opening or in the middle game. But, in the end game the side that has the cleanest plan/method to get a clear advantage wins the game. In the end game you must think if I had 4 moves right after another, what would I do? What would warrant a win for me? What's the win condition that if met, I'll have a definite advantage and win. Find a sequence of moves that achieves a clear goal or advantage. Think in terms of your opponent's weaknesses and how to attack them. Or if there are no weaknesses, try to provoke them to make weakening moves and then attack the weaknesses. The more committed your opponent's moves are, the more chances you have in finding soft spots in their position.

Many times, especially in end game scenarios all you have to do is nothing but wait so the opponent runs out of good moves and is forced into making self harm (zugzwang). It's important to know how to do nothing, when the time is right.

LIFE PRINCIPLE #26

Doing a "Pass move" is when you try to make a quiet move to pass the tempo (time) and leave it to your opponent to move and potentially weaken their position.

"Just defended" is defended. Sometimes when under attack you can defend your opponent's threat and their attack can't proceed anymore. In that case you have successfully defended the position and are not required to add to defense anymore. Adding more defenses than necessary is bad because that piece could potentially be used in an attack, but you've decided to unnecessarily bring it to defense of a situation which is sufficiently defended already. If a situation is defended, don't add more defenses. If it's just defended, that's enough.

It's very important to distinguish between a threat by your opponent and a move which looks threatening but in fact is not a threat, but overextension. When facing a threatening move, it's imperative to analyze the move deep enough to know whether it creates a real threat or it's in fact not a good move for them. If their move (regardless of how threatening it looks) is easily defendable or can be stopped, you must respond to it based on the correct evaluation.

If a threat is in fact not a big threat, you should not respond to it as a threat, but you can ignore it and carry on with your plan. If you evaluate their move to be a mistake, find the best punishment for it.

Wait and bait. If nothing else is to be done, improve your position or bait your opponent to make a bad move or a concession, any type of it and then punish their mistake in the best possible way. Wait in the dark like a predator waiting for their prey. The predator has tracked the prey for some time now and knows its habits and escape routes. So, he waits until the prey is in the most vulnerable position and then strikes. Entice the opponent to overextend and create weakness or problem for themselves.

CHAPTER 10

STRATEGIC MINDSET

CHAPTER 10
STRATEGIC MINDSET

If you are materially ahead (let's say up-the-exchange), it's in your favor to trade down your pieces, simplify the position and enter the end-game, unless you have an opportunity to checkmate sooner. Material advantage gets more prominent when more pieces are off the board. In the end game having an extra pawn could be the difference between win and loss.

LIFE PRINCIPLE #27

If you are ahead, simplify the situation. If not, complicate it.

You are expected to win a game if you have a decisive advantage. Converting a winning position into a win is a must have skill.

LIFE PRINCIPLE #28

If you are lucky or have access to more resources or worked into an advantageous situation, you're expected to be more successful in life. It is also a responsibility.

If your opponent attacks in the center, attack them on the flanks and vice versa.

LIFE PRINCIPLE #29

Distract your opponent by getting them into battlefields which they are not ready for.

Knowing patterns (known positions and tactics) from beforehand is extremely important. There are well-known checkmating patterns that you need to master. These patterns play an important role in the way we play the game, you may be able to see glimpses of those end-game patterns in the middle game. We either detect these patterns on the board and act according to our previous knowledge, or we change the course of the game towards a position that is similar to a known pattern to be in our favor. The more patterns you know, the more knowledge you have over your opponent.

LIFE PRINCIPLE #30

Knowing phrases to use or the way to handle things from personal or other's experience is very useful. The more exposure you have to similar situations, the better prepared you will get. Learn as much as possible from beforehand about any situation that is likely to happen.

Knowing the Next move is very powerful; what's done/committed by both sides is already on the board. You have to predict your opponent's next move (or possible next moves that make sense for them) and devise plans accordingly. Also if you have a sequence of moves in your head (a line) and you already know your next move, that's great.

"The most powerful weapon in Chess is to have the next move."

– GM David Bronstein

However, don't just automatically play your candidate next move right after the opponent moves their piece, recalculate again and check the validity of the plan (again), especially if the opponent doesn't play the best move for themselves. Some of your opponent's moves may change the situation in a way that you have to change your next move in response to what they are doing. For example, if they created a new threat with their recent move and if you don't do anything you're going to lose material because of it, you must first address the risk, unless your attack results in checkmate.

LIFE PRINCIPLE #31

**At any given time you have to have calculated
the critical lines ahead and if required
play based on those plans, very fast.**

Sacrifices for both sides have to be calculated and the end position evaluated correctly. Sound sacrifices must be taken on time. Unsound sacrifices should be ignored or kept in mind for the future, where they may become a valid plan or stay invalid.

Never let an opponent who is materially down take the initiative. When you're ahead (material, initiative, space control, tempo) you need to continue going forward and continue being ahead and dominating the board. Don't exchange down and don't retreat into a defensive position when you're ahead. Always be as aggressive as possible and go forward. Any time that you become complacent, your position takes a hit and can lose the advantage easily this way. Not taking a good chance is just like losing pieces or tempi.

When calculating lines and exchanges, think of what remains on the board. The end position is important, not what comes off the board.

Restrict the movement of your opponent's king by taking squares beside him, from him. This is done by checking those squares. Learn the most famous end-games patterns and mating nets *(e.g. back-rank mate, smothered mate, Anastasia mate, arabian mate, etc.)*

LIFE PRINCIPLE #32

**Learn from masters on how they finish off their
opponent at the later stages of an encounter. End
is the most important aspect of everything. How
you leave a relationship (even bad ones) has a
big effect on the evaluation and effect of it.**

Always look for trapping your opponent's pieces, if possible. It's an easy way of gaining advantage. Don't be materialistic and take all sacrifices (including queen sacs, rook sacs, piece sac or a pawn sac) into consideration and calculate them. Many times, when your position is good, you can afford to sacrifice, but come out as the winner.

If you have such an opportunity and don't use it, it'll most likely backfire later when you fall behind for the very reason.

If simplification is in your favor, do it. This could mean fixing your opponent's pawns on non-optimal squares making them targets for future phases of the game. Backward pawns and isolated pawns are perfect targets. You may still be unable to attack them, but fixing them on weak squares will keep them weak until you can attack them.

Checks, captures and threats should be calculated on each move, for both sides, in this order. Always be aware of your opponent's threats too. If it can become a serious threat, try to diffuse it efficiently. Don't use half measures because if you weaken your position (while thinking you're diffusing the threats) your position can deteriorate rapidly. Be cautious of pushing the pawns in front of a castled king, these pawns are best untouched, however a pushed middle pawn with a fianchetto bishop is a strong defense for a king. Especially if a knight accompanies them.

If a move is good to go, always do it immediately and don't lose time preparing a move which is already good to go. Tempo is of the essence and you can get behind if not using your turn with a powerful move and waste it with a weak move. Try to build a solid position that has less weaknesses (targets, weak spots) than your opponent and poses more threats than your opponent.

Targets and weak spots become extremely important in an end-game. Backward pawns, restricted pieces, outposts and other weak spots in your opponent's camp should be detected or even encouraged to be created by your moves. Coordinate your moves so they are forced to make weakening moves which you can further utilize to increase the pressure. Almost always, when you stay calm, play solidly and increase the pressure, they eventually blunder.

"Weak points or holes in the opponent's position must be occupied by pieces not Pawns."

— *Siegbert Tarrasch*

Always keep the long term strategy in mind but complement it with tactics. Regardless of long term strategy, for each stage of the game have a goal in mind i.e., Long term strategy is to attack the king on the king-side, but in the interim there's an attack in the center that needs attention and I have to be able to diffuse it efficiently, block every threat and then attack the king.

Discovered attacks are very effective. Double attacks and especially double checks are extremely effective. Always look for doubling the effects. In most cases if the opponent can't move a pinned piece, they will struggle even more. Don't trade down just yet. Increase the pressure and you'll eventually win the pinned piece. If you attack pre-maturely you'll also lose the tempo of the game because you can't follow up your attack. Your attack must be done at a time which is effective. Not one move earlier or later than required. There will be more margin for error if you are early or late, i.e. it is best to act right on time, but if you can't get the timing absolutely right it's better to be early than late.

When there's 3 pawns besides each other, attack the one in the middle. Pawns are good in chains and are strong when supporting each other in progressing forward. It's best to break pawn chains.

Many times the break-through move comes by attacking the most protected square. This is not a hard and fast rule that works all the time, but in many situations that you think you have developed and improved your position as much as possible and it's time to break the position, it happens to work. Many times it's best to attack the most protected square. This is a way of calling off your opponent's bluff and telling them I'm going to break you where you think is your strongest point. You have to be cocky and arrogant (only in your head) with your moves. Moves should be daring in Chess and life, if you've calculated precisely.

"Ask yourself: Why must I lose to this idiot?"

— *Aron Nimzovich*

LIFE PRINCIPLE #33

Sometimes it's best to attack your opponent where they think they are strong, safe and most protected. Proving their strong point to be weak is a very effective strategy. If you have the chance to attack their strong point, don't waste time and resources attacking a minor weakness.

If you find an advantage in any form, try to add the same type of advantage, it's very likely that adding the same type of pressure can lead to a clear advantage down the track. Focus on your strengths. If you have space advantage, continue with the same ideas to build upon and increase that space advantage. If you're ahead in development, try to develop even further and hinder their development.

Add to the pressure step by step. Don't cash-in too early and don't release the pressure before its perfect time. Wait as long as necessary and not one move less or more. Only release the tension when you know an exchange is going to yield considerable advantage in the resulting position.

One of the most important aspects of the game is the order/sequence of moves. A move may look attractive, but you have to wait until it's time to execute it. Early/premature execution of a plan leads to a half-baked attack. Sometimes the moves are the same, you just change their order and it makes sense now. A different sequence of moves (even though moves are the same) is a completely different line and have to be evaluated separately. The order of moves is as important as the move itself.

In-between moves must be considered and calculated precisely. Sometimes the position is so complex that in the middle of the line, there might be an in-between move (most of the time it's a forcing move, like a check) that saves a piece from being captured or captures an additional piece. If you don't calculate and execute the in-between move, you haven't gained any advantage from that line. But if you can find, calculate and execute the in-between moves, it'll yield an advantage.

Think hard on your moves and use your time wisely. Think even harder when it's your opponent's turn. Use their time to your advantage. This is a super important factor: Don't get complacent. When it's not your opponent's turn to move, it doesn't mean you have free time to lose or rest. It means you get time with less stress to think (and out-think your opponent). Study and analyze the position and come up with a plan and calculate the probable lines ahead.

When you improve the position up to a point where you can hardly find any ideas for improvement, look for triggering breaks and exchanges. When your position is good chances of sacrifice or tricks show up.

Learn to think and act like a master. A master's moves may look suicidal to untrained eye, but because it's always calculated to yield results, it's ok. A sacrifice is justified if your end position is superior and you have calculated the continuation precisely.

If your opponent makes a committing move *(e.g. pushing a pawn forward)* try to think about the ways to diffuse it. Many times when you're being attacked, you are able to blockade their attack and change the position into one that can only benefit you in the long run, because their attack is blocked and now it's only you who can push for victory. They have committed and their attack is diffused. If you properly diffuse an upcoming attack, it's like being materially ahead. It's a sort of small victory to successfully parry an attack and completely shut it down. It shows you're in charge of the position and know how to deal with their attack. Hopefully they are not as ready when you're going to attack them.

If you are playing against multiple opponents *(i.e. a simultaneous chess game)* you have to find out who plays strongly and assign more time to those games and less time to easier opponents. Assigning time wisely between the games is also critical. Don't focus all your attention on a particular game, if you've got several of them being played at the same time. Assign more time to games with stronger players.

Being able to force your opponent into an exchange is a sign of a strong position (meaning the alternative would be worse for them so they are forced into the exchange). If you're the one calling the shots and forcing your opponent into doing something because alternative is worse for them, it means they are forced to make your move, otherwise their position deteriorates. Most of the time, that exchange is non-optimal for them too and eventually leads to them falling behind. The side that makes the threats, keeps checking, capturing and making threats almost always wins. The side that has to parry the attacks, make defensive measures and forced into unfavorable exchanges, has the lower hand.

Regardless of all the calculations and analysis, the only thing that matters is your next move. It's good to have the line in your head, but it starts with the next move.

Value of an advantage increases the later it is in the game. Being a piece up in the opening is less important than being a pawn up in the end-game.

> *"After a bad opening, there is hope for the middle game. After a bad middle game, there is hope for the endgame. But once you are in the endgame, the moment of truth has arrived."*
>
> — *Edmar Mednis*

Also the impact of a mistake increases the later it is in the game. If you make mistakes in the opening, there is still time and pieces on the board to create new tricks and threats. But, if you make a mistake in the end-game you're most likely will lose that game because the chances of countering becomes much less.

> *"A Chess game is a dialogue, a conversation between a player and his opponent. Each move by the opponent may contain threats or be a blunder, but a player cannot defend against threats or take advantage of blunders if he does not first ask himself: What is my opponent planning after each move?"*
>
> — *Edmar Mednis*

Ask yourself about the opponent's best plan of action, after each move. What are they trying to do? You need to think from your opponent's perspective as well as yours. You have to be able to rotate the chess board in your head and place yourself in the opponent's place and think instead of them and find the best move for them. What are they trying to achieve with their last move? What is their plan? Is it a legitimate threat? Does it require any action? If so, how can I diffuse it?

Playing rapid or blitz games (anything less than 15 minutes per side) has a very bad effect on your progress in chess. Apart from solving puzzles the only online games which are useful for your chess skills is correspondence mode. In correspondence each side has at least 24 hours to make their move. You can play 20 to 50 correspondence games at the same time.

The benefit of correspondence chess is that you play against humans, but each side has lots of time to think and make their move. This gives you enough time to think all you want about the position and make the best move you think you can come up with.

Correspondence mode has a very good effect on your mind, especially when you play more than 10 games at the same time: You keep remembering positions: Oh, this is the game where I lost a pawn in the opening. In this one I've lost the queen for a rook, but I'm still battling ahead. This helps your imagination and remembering skills. To remember your lines, keeping them all in your head. I suggest you visit your online correspondence games no more than 3 times a day, but each time spend enough time to move all the games ahead at the same time.

Changes in the balance of power are usually limited in any given game. This means if you're ahead, you can keep being ahead by playing solidly and you're expected to win because of that advantage. If you don't play accurately you can lose your advantage and it'll be your opponent who has the upper hand and is expected to win. It's unlikely for the balance of power to change hands several times during each game, but this happens more on the lower level games: both sides make lots of mistakes and the side which can detect it sooner and exploit it, wins.

In the high caliber games where both sides know how to play accurately and solidly, the side that blunders or even makes a mistake first, pays for it by losing the game. But in a game between two rookie players it can happen that one side makes a mistake and gives the advantage to the other side until the other side makes a mistake and gives the power back to the first side. However, the number of times the advantageous side gives it away to the other side is usually limited. It's highly unlikely to lose and gain the advantage several times in a game. If you have the advantage you must keep it and increase it. If you're behind, you must close the gap and reduce their advantage by playing accurate moves.

This is a very strong concept: you can make intentional concessions in areas that are very hard for your opponent to exploit that specific retreat. In many traditional openings white—who is up a tempo—brings out pieces and develops with tempo if possible and it is black's responsibility to respond to each one of those punches with counter measures. Sveshnikov is a variation in Sicilian opening that is black who conducts the aggression. In Sveshniko, black at the cost of some early positional concessions has a very dynamic play. Black's clear advantage is that they have the upper hand in entering the end game at any given time by initiating massive exchanges.

In this opening black should be very tactically aware as the uncastelled white king can get into trouble. This is a brilliant play style especially when you're behind materially or in development. You create weaknesses in your position which (hopefully) your opponent doesn't know how to exploit. Utilizing and exploiting those weaknesses requires very accurate play by your opponent. They need to know exactly how to exploit it, otherwise they can't. In this opening you play aggressive annoying moves on each move as black.

Svenshnikov showcases a very specific and strong style of play with strategic concessions at the start, but those concessions are not easy to exploit. With openings like this, you create weaknesses in your position, but exploiting them is not easy, unless your opponent knows exactly what to do so early on, otherwise it is only you who can get ahead with a very dynamic position.

In Sveshnikov the white side has some chances to get ahead, but they don't find it most of the time! Sveshnikov is an example of an early positional concession system which is also sound. With this type of dynamic play, black creates early intentional concessions which results in a very dynamic play giving black opportunities to strike early on or have the trigger in their hand when they want to enter an easy endgame. This is a brilliant style of play and you should always think in terms of early planned concessions which are hard to exploit but give you a dynamic position with lots of opportunities and better chances.

Some of these strategies are based on the fact that exploiting the concession rarely happens, because human blind spots stops the other side from detecting it as a concession or finding out how to utilize that concession.

LIFE PRINCIPLE #34

A strategic/intentional retreat in certain areas, especially early on, can be an effective method. The other side needs to be very precise to find the refutation to your concessions and act on it which is not easy to do especially at the start where options are more.

This strategic retreat may be in the shape of showing weakness in an aspect which is not very critical to your main objectives, i.e. finding an aspect to be humble about, but that aspect needs to be non-critical for example you may choose to not play in one side of the board and seemingly allow the opponent to take more control of that side, but knowing that it's ok because it's not easy for them to convert that space advantage into a decisive advantage.

If you're going to use this method you should choose the aspect you retreat to very wisely, i.e. the part you are taking intentional concessions should be meaningless for your overall plan and it should be hard for your opponent to find the refutation of those concessions.

This intentional concession is made with the intention of 1) keeping the opponent busy at the start and making them think and lose their time (because of your unorthodox opening approach) and 2) allowing you to deliver your main objective in another aspect (which is the critical aspect in your plan).

When you don't see a good way forward or you feel your position is getting under pressure, you can change the structure of the position. This can be done with the push of pawns forward. Pawn pushes usually change the structure of the position in many ways: Squares/pieces which were protected before, become vulnerable. Pawn pushes also can bring a bad bishop to life by opening its diagonal or rendering a good bishop useless by blocking its diagonal.

Sometimes moving the same piece several times in the opening can get an advantage, but most of the time it's bad to move the same piece more than once in the opening because it means you're neglecting developing other pieces.

Think of yourself as a military commander with an army of pieces that you can utilize to cripple the opponent's army from development. You must think of the seriousness of each threat and assess moves and positions correctly. If a move is bad for your opponent, utilize it, exploit it, make it worse for them.

Pawns have a very strong feature that if they remain in the game and can be pushed all the way to the other side, they promote to whatever piece they like. This is a very special feature of the end-games. Passed pawns (pawns on empty file that can not be harrased by enemy pawns) mush be pushed as soon as possible. Put a rook behind passed pawns(whether it's yours or the enemy's). When promoting think of which piece will deliver the desired result. Most of the times promoting to queen makes sense, but sometimes it may be beneficial to use the geometry of pieces and promote to a rook, bishop or even knight. Calculate each line and evaluate the end position in your head. Choose the best line.

CHAPTER 11

VICIOUS PREDATOR MINDSET

CHAPTER 11
VICIOUS PREDATOR MINDSET

The aim is to make the most powerful moves that make your opponent desperate and encourage them to resign as early as possible. Don't get complacent, if you're having a comfortable game and position. In each move the most powerful one should be calculated, found and selected. This is always the move sequence that leads to checkmate, so if there's a shorter checkmate, you must choose that line.

Everything in chess is measurable, each move is better or worse than the other one. You choose the moves. Choose wisely.

LIFE PRINCIPLE #35

**Only make strong actions, no half measures.
Always show up, be professional, be your best and
strongest and don't show weakness of any kind.**

**If there's a better way of being or doing, do that. Get
out of bad mindset in a heartbeat (like a Ninja).**

Always sweep the board for changes that create new tactical threats for you and your opponent. Always look for weaknesses.

The proper mentality to win games is to think and act like a vicious predator that's going to kill the opponent one way or another, or gets killed itself trying to beat you. No time to waste, no concessions, no complacency, no defensive mindset. Increase the pressure and attack whenever possible and try to gain as much advantage as soon as possible in any shape or form. When not possible to attack, improve your position incrementally and build a solid position to attack later. When required to defend, do so with everything in your power to turn the tables and get on the front foot again: Better position so we can attack again. Reserve every resource— especially time and brain power— for as late as possible, because you're going to need it in the end-game. If played sound and well by both sides, the opening and middle game should be balanced. Most of the result will be determined in the end-game, unless one side makes an inaccuracy/mistake/blunder in the opening or middle game. Become a vicious predator that never steps back, fights back even if injured and pushed into a disadvantage. Even in a dead-lost situation a vicious attacker never gives up and looks for opportunities to equalize and even get ahead.

LIFE PRINCIPLE #36

Resilience is the best mentality to develop. Nothing should discourage you. Even if you're in deep trouble and the position seems hopeless you still have to make the best moves.

It's best to not respond aggressively to provocative moves. Your job is always to find the best sound move and avoid emotional moves. If your opponent's move is bad or unexpected for you, you must analyze it and act accordingly.

If your opponent's move is provocative, try to not act aggressively and continue playing sound chess.

LIFE PRINCIPLE #37

System 1 thinking (knee-jerk reaction) is very bad for decision making most of the time. You need to rely on logic and calculation (system 2 thinking) more than system 1.

CHAPTER 12

ANTIFRAGILITY MINDSET

CHAPTER 12
ANTIFRAGILITY MINDSET

The aim is to make the most powerful moves that make your opponent desperate and encourage them to resign as early as possible. Don't get complacent, if you're having a comfortable game and position. In each move the most powerful one should be calculated, found and selected. This is always the move sequence that leads to checkmate, so if there's a shorter checkmate, you must choose that line.

Everything in chess is measurable, each move is better or worse than the other one. You choose the moves. Choose wisely.

LIFE PRINCIPLE #35

**Only make strong actions, no half measures.
Always show up, be professional, be your best and
strongest and don't show weakness of any kind.**

**If there's a better way of being or doing, do that. Get
out of bad mindset in a heartbeat (like a Ninja).**

Always sweep the board for changes that create new tactical threats for you and your opponent. Always look for weaknesses.

The proper mentality to win games is to think and act like a vicious predator that's going to kill the opponent one way or another, or gets killed itself trying to beat you. No time to waste, no concessions, no complacency, no defensive mindset. Increase the pressure and attack whenever possible and try to gain as much advantage as soon as possible in any shape or form. When not possible to attack, improve your position incrementally and build a solid position to attack later. When required to defend, do so with everything in your power to turn the tables and get on the front foot again: Better position so we can attack again. Reserve every resource (especially time and brain power) for as late as possible, because you're going to need it in the end-game. If played sound and well by both sides, the opening and middle game should be balanced. Most of the result will be determined in the end-game, unless one side makes an inaccuracy/mistake/blunder in the opening or middle game. Become a vicious predator that never steps back, fights back even if injured and pushed into a disadvantage. Even in a dead-lost situation a vicious attacker never gives up and looks for opportunities to equalize and even get ahead.

LIFE PRINCIPLE #36

**Resilience is the best mentality to develop.
Nothing should discourage you. Even if you're in
deep trouble and the position seems hopeless
you still have to make the best moves.**

It's best to not respond aggressively to provocative moves. Your job is always to find the best sound move and avoid emotional moves. If your opponent's move is bad or unexpected for you, you must analyze it and act accordingly.

If your opponent's move is provocative, try to not act aggressively and continue playing sound chess.

LIFE PRINCIPLE #37

**System 1 thinking (knee-jerk reaction) is very
bad for decision making most of the time.
You need to rely on logic and calculation
(system 2 thinking) more than system 1.**

CHAPTER 13

TUG OF WAR
BETWEEN CHESS PIECES

CHAPTER 13
TUG OF WAR BETWEEN CHESS PIECES

Each move changes the balance of power in one way or another. Chess and life are complex and each move changes the dynamics and introduces new chances, weaknesses and threats for both sides. Study the gaps in your opponent's position and try to utilize weak spots or provoke a bad/weakening move by them.

LIFE PRINCIPLE #39

Each action, even if it looks threatening, will change the situation in a way that may offer you opportunities.

Apart from finding the best action for yourself, look into weaknesses of your competitors and use those to your advantage to come up with plans.

Think of a chess game like a game of tug of War between white and black army.

At the beginning, the tie is in the middle and the game is balanced. When a side plays better (in terms of accuracy) the tie moves in their favor and their position becomes stronger. If the other side can push back and get to equality, then they can push for a win, but if they continue playing badly their position deteriorates. If one side makes a mistake or blunders the tie moves against them significantly, however if the other side doesn't manage to exploit that mistake, then the tie comes to the middle again.

This is why it's crucial to analyze each move of the opponent to check if it's a bad move and needs to be punished. Not only that but you have to guess the best move for your opponent on each turn. If they play based on your expectations, you already calculated the lines and know how to play it, but if they play a move which surprises you and you didn't expect it, it's quite probable that its a bad move for them (because you already calculated their best move). Sometimes however, their move might reveal new tricks (that you didn't see earlier).

It's not sufficient to play good strong moves for yourself, but you need to respond to the situation on the board and the opponent's moves, if it's a bad move, punish it and if it's a good one that you didn't expect, correct your calculations.

LIFE PRINCIPLE #40

Advantages are built incrementally, each precise move counts. Especially if it can work as part of a bigger plan.

CHAPTER 14

ART OF WAR

CHAPTER 14
ART OF WAR

The best general rule is to play your pieces forward. If you move a piece backwards, it almost always comes with some sort of concession on your side that your opponent can potentially use. Coming back is a concession in one way or another. Moving a piece backwards changes the balance against you, most of the time. Of course, there are exceptions: for defense, for a longer-term plan, to deceive your opponent, a decoy, etc. But it's mostly rare that a move backward could be good. Default should be to push forward, restrict the opponent from free development and control more space. Add pressure and improve your position until it's time to strike.

Moving forward and restricting the opponent's pieces and especially checking the squares around their king is the way to victory. This is why pawns only move forward; other pieces are also meant to be pushed forward, at least most of the time.

LIFE PRINCIPLE #41

The best advice is to think forward and move ahead. You may retreat in some areas intentionally for longer-term goals, but the general theme should be to move forward (especially towards the center), adding pressure and restricting your opponent's moves.

There are 3 game phases, each having its own characteristics and general set of rules:

Opening: The aim is to use a minimum amount of time to control the center and develop your pieces and deploy your army into meaningful squares in a way that they are coordinated and support each other for a future plan of attack. Opening Has strict rules and known patterns. There are some opening tricks and gambits that your opponent can use to checkmate you very quickly, 2 examples are fried liver attack and legal mate. Be aware of most of them and avoid opening tricks if you can. The aim of the opening is to use minimal time and make standard moves to take as much space as possible, accept no concessions, play solidly, don't waste time and lead the opening into a healthy middle game. It is ideal to have clear plans for the middle game from the opening, however, this is not always possible especially if your opponent plays well or knows that opening very well from before. In the opening usually both players play known moves (book moves) up to a point where one side diverges from book moves.

Middle Game: A couple of pieces have been traded and there may be gaps and opportunities in some areas of the board. You're expected to find a solid plan to increase your advantage. There may be some trading opportunities that can result in the end game. These opportunities need to be assessed individually, if the resulting end game will be in our favor, we will initiate the exchange and follow the plan. With fewer pieces on the board, gaps and opportunities arise on both sides and you can benefit from them. Also, have to keep a close eye on threats and plan defense accordingly. Plans need to be calculated beforehand and in your head, because your time is getting tighter. Be careful with committing moves *(e.g. castles or pushing pawns)* because you've made it clear where your king will be and it'll be easier for your opponent to attack the king. Try to keep your options open and the position fluid, for as long as you can, e.g. keep both options open to castle short or long, for as long as you can.

End game: Most pieces are traded down and your options and plans— as well as your opponent's— are reduced. Options for both sides are reduced and the ultimate plan for both sides is more or less clear. You need to execute your best plan and try to checkmate your opponent quicker than them, while keeping an eye on your king's defense at the same time and defusing your opponent's threats.

LIFE PRINCIPLE #42

Each encounter has three phases:

Opening: Options are limitless and risks are lower at the start. Be aware of decision making or strong commitments at this stage. Act standardly and quickly. Don't waste time. Play Ok and good moves and lead into a balanced middle game.

Middle: More information is revealed by both sides and plans ahead get more clear for both sides. Keep the position fluid and flexible for as long as possible.

End: Need to reach the end goals quicker than the opponent. Quicker here doesn't refer to time, but it means before they can come up with a counterattack.

The process to calculate each line is as follows:

Step 1: Consequences of your opponent's last move

1.1. Does their move attack something? (direct threat)

1.2. How are other pieces influenced by their move? (indirect threats)

1.3. What weaknesses does their move leave behind?

Step 2: Finding candidate moves

2.1. Do I have any tactical opportunities to get an advantage? (Checks/Captures/Threats, undefended pieces)

2.2. If not, how can I improve my position?

Step 3: Blunder check

3.1. Can the piece I am about to move be captured or harassed? (direct threats)

3.2. How will other pieces be influenced by my move? (indirect threats)

3.3. What weaknesses does my move leave behind?

You must develop the discipline to repeat the steps above before making each move. This method is the way to apply your brain power to any chess position. You first analyze the opponent's last move (or couple of moves) to find weaknesses (direct or indirect). Then you find your best candidate moves(to respond to their weakness or improve the position of your pieces). Finally you double check for blunders, does the move you're about to play have a clear refutation by your opponent?

Tempo is the name of the game: Chess is all about tempo. Tempo is when you can force the rhythm of the game. Tempo could be forced (check) or optional (capture, threats). It's best to create a sound in your head which helps you to calculate lines better. Many use the sound "Tac". This means you say tac in between your moves and follow the line as quickly as possible. For example: rook, tac(and move the rook to the square in your head), bishop, tac, their bishop, tac. You get the idea. You can replace tac with any other sound that works for you, but many found tac to be the nicest chess queue as it sounds like when the sword touches the armor. When you are checking the opponent king, you are in fact using the sword of your pieces. There's a lot of benefits to see chess like this: Pawns are the weakest chess piece individually and they only have daggers, not even swords! Knights have swords and bishops have arrows. Rooks have strong swords and Queen has a very strong battle axe. King is defenseless and can only walk. Queen and bishops are fast and knights can jump.

When a piece moves to a square— especially if it's a check or capture)— it's like your piece is creating a sound (tac) while doing so. It's like pieces attack each other with a sword or arrow and the sound is tac. This sound helps you to calculate lines very quickly. Move the pieces in your mind and say tac in between. Try to evaluate and compare each end position resulting from each line.

APPENDIX
CHESS EXAMPLES

1. Center of the board is the 4 green squares. Red squares are side-central squares. The more control you have over these squares, the better your play will be. Control means having them under attack with any piece or better having your pieces in these squares.

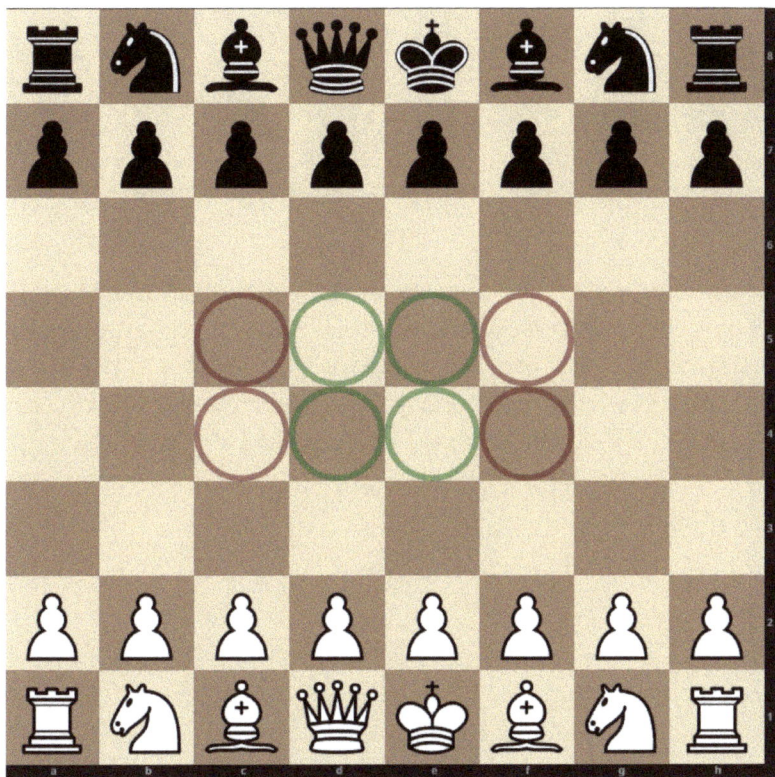

Fig. 1

For example, see position #2 below:

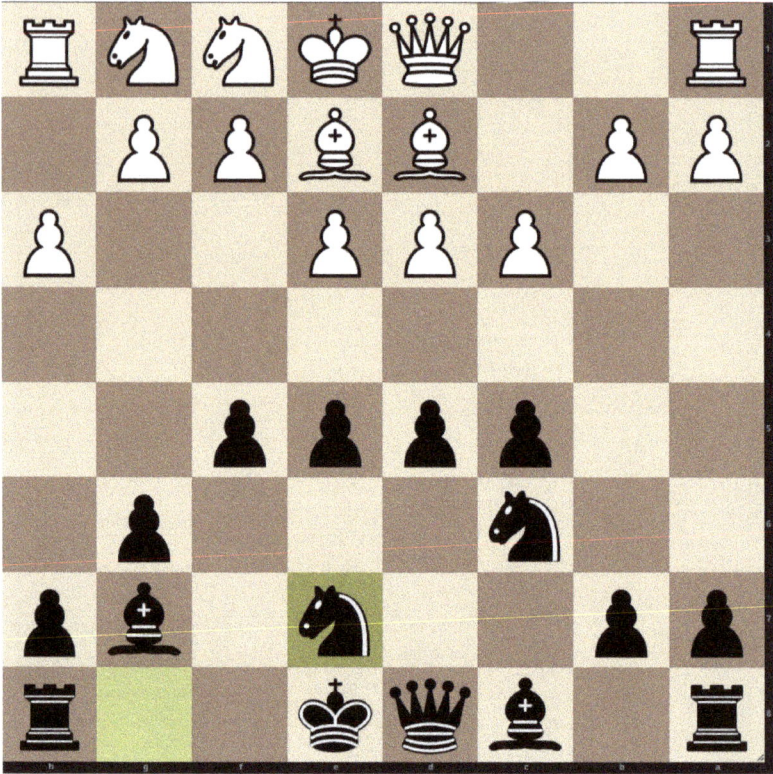

Fig. 2

Black has dominated the central squares while white has played very unambitiously and left the central control. Black has managed to plant 2 pawns in the center (d5 and e5) and also two pawns in the side central squares (c5 and f5) while white has no pieces in those important central squares. The central domination by black will result in an easier play and win against a passive setup by white. Black can choose to push any of the pawns, at any time.

2. In below position whites' best move is c4, contesting the center.

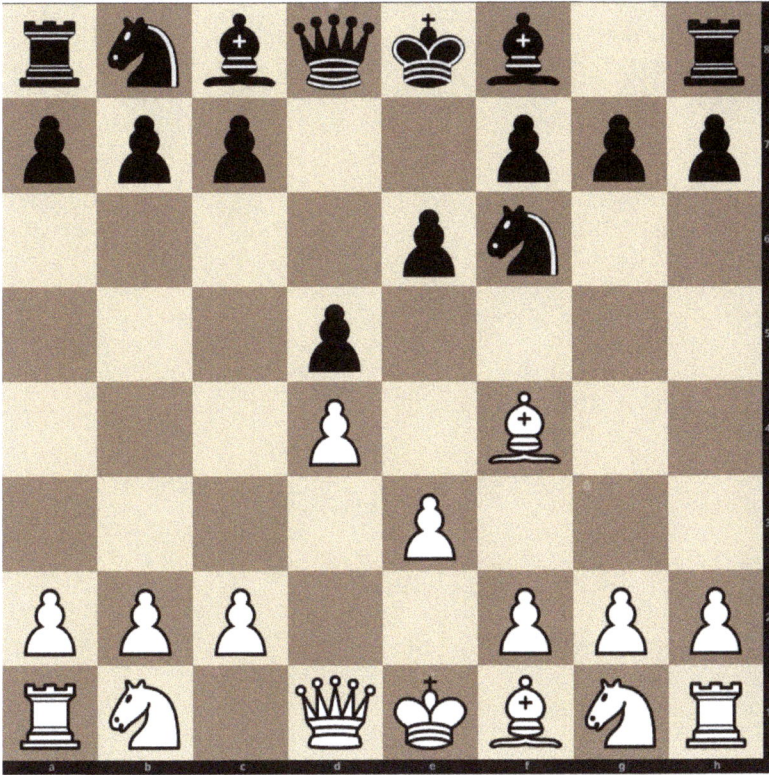

Fig. 3

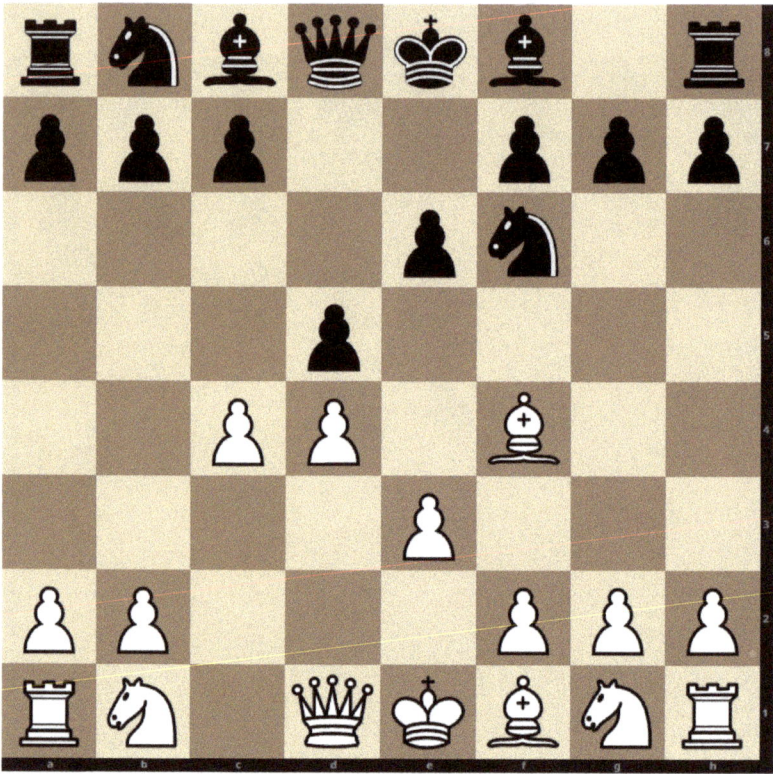

Fig. 4

Black should NOT take the c4 pawn because the resulting position (see position #5 below) is worse for black. If black takes the c4 pawn they have exchanged their central pawn with a side central pawn of white which is bad for black. When calculating exchanges look for what remains on the board after the exchange and pay no attention to what comes off the board. You'll be forced to play with what's on the board, this is why the pieces and the position that remains is important. The tension between pawns on d5 and c4 should not be released by either side, unless there's a clear advantage to be gained from it. In this case black should not take the pawn on c4 because it will develop white's bishop for free, without wasting a tempo.

Also it's not in white's favor to release the tension because no clear advantage can be obtained from the exchange. If white decides to take the d5 pawn black can take back with knight which centralizes the knight, comes with an attack on f4 bishop and no gain for white. It's best for both sides to keep the tension and not release yet.

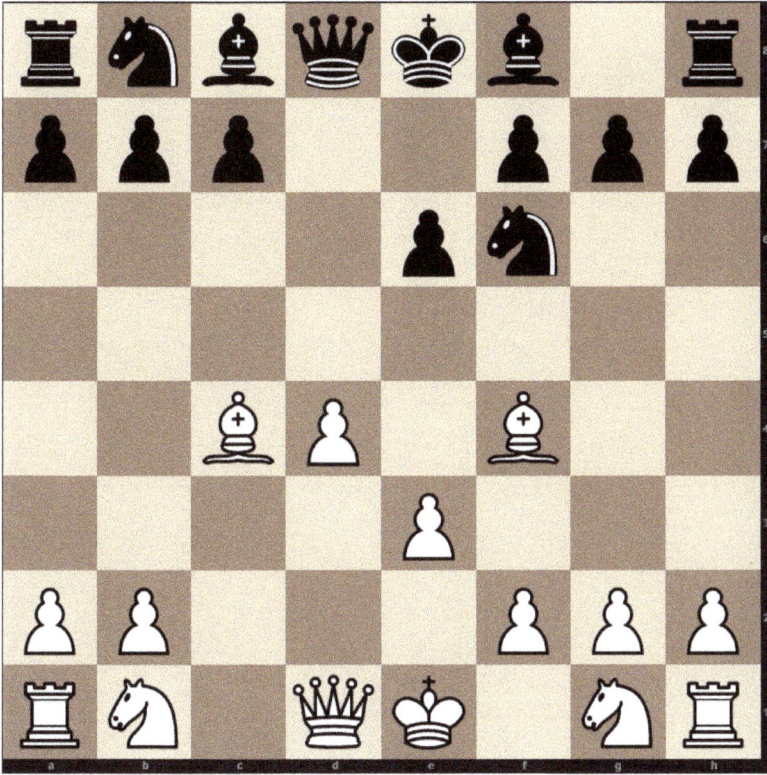

Fig. 5

After postion #4, black's best move is to play C5 contesting the central pawn of white on C4 while clearing the C6 square for their knight to be developed to.

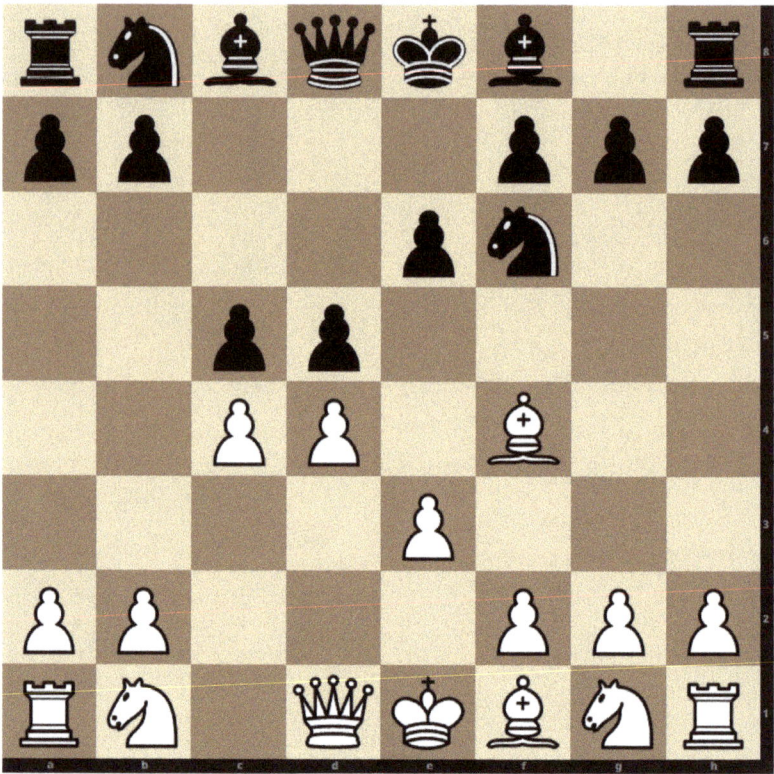

Fig. 6

If black plays Nc6 before pushing the pawn to C5, the knight will be blocking the pawn to be pushed forward. This is why it's best for the pawn to be pushed first and then develop the knight behind it.

3. Tactical awareness is crucial in chess. In the below position, it's black to play. What is the threat of black that must be detected and neutralized by white?

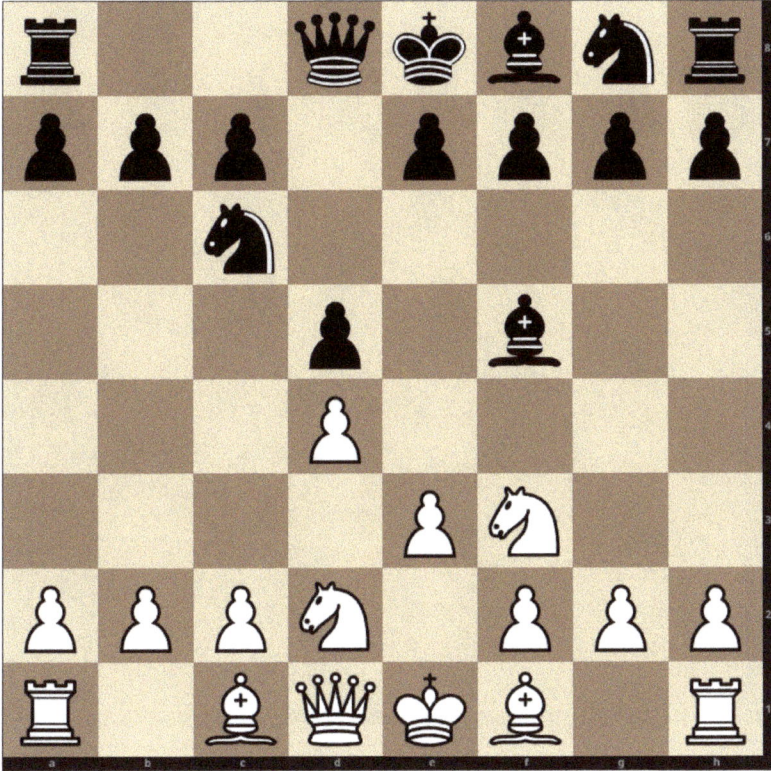

Fig. 7

If you found Nb4, you're correct. If black gets to play Nb4 they can play Nxc2+ on the next move, forking the king and rook on a1. See below:

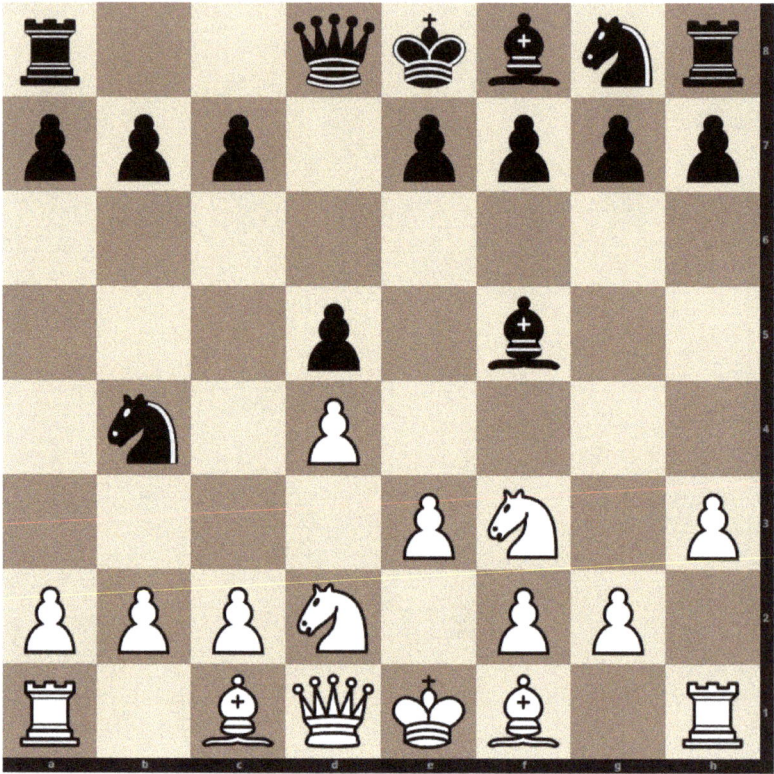

Fig. 8

Fig. 9

Knight is supported by the bishop on f5, so the queen doesn't want to sacrifice herself (9 points) for a knight (3 points). If you are playing white, you must be aware of this tactic and play a2 on time, disallowing knight to jump to b4 in the first place. Below is the correct play for white after position #7. What you allow is as important as what you do. You should not allow the knight to jump to b4. Pawn push to a3 is to disallow Nb4.

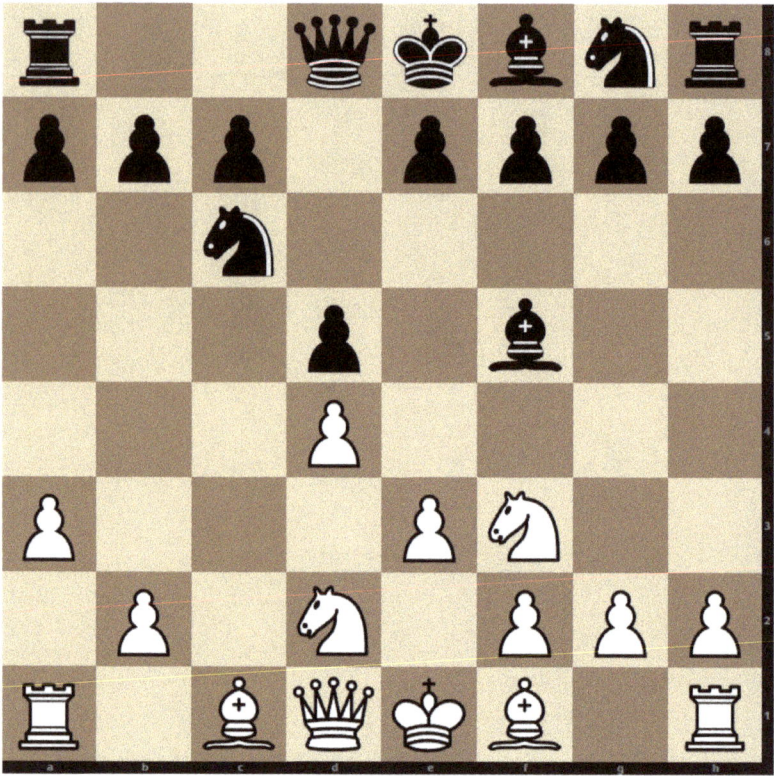

Fig. 10

4. In below position it's white to play. Is it possible/good for white to take the pawn on a6 or not?

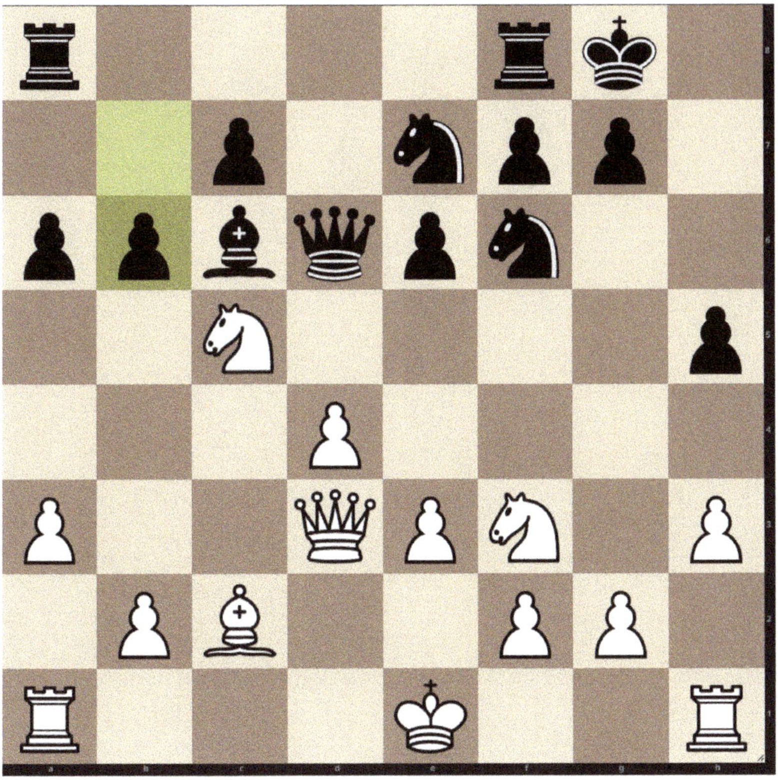

Fig. 11

The answer is no, it's too greedy for white to take the pawn, especially with an uncastled king in the middle of the board. Let's say white decides to take the pawn:

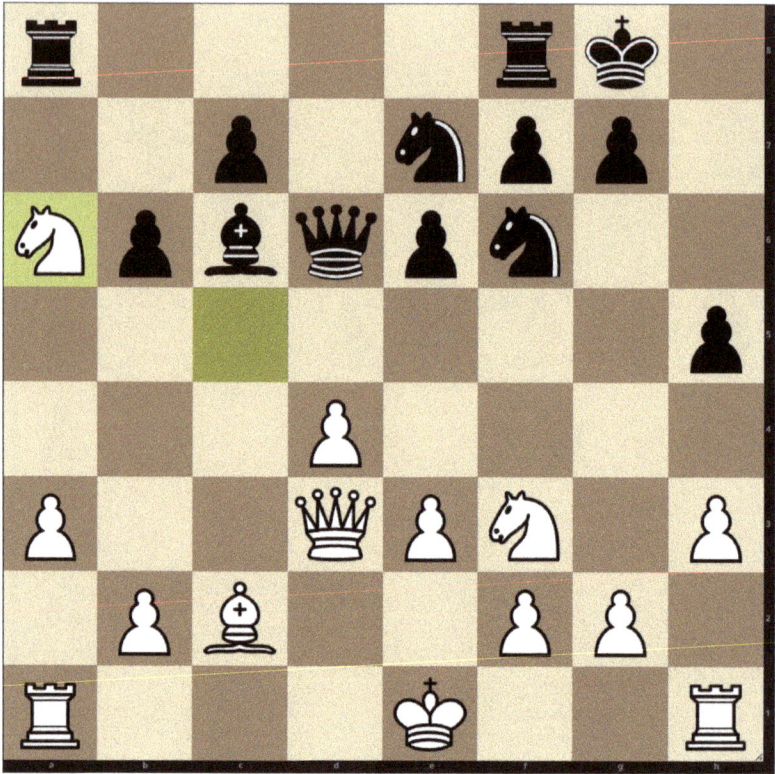

Fig. 12

What would be the best response for black? What's the correct tactic by black to win a piece? Did you find Bf5?

Fig. 13

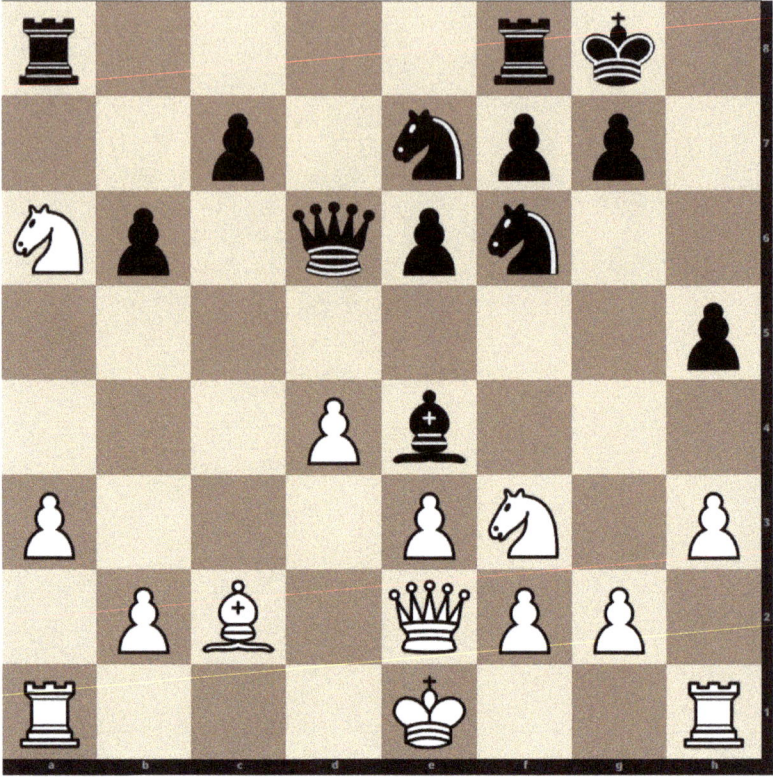

Fig. 14

With Qe2 white tries their best to defend both bishop on c2 and knight on a3, but black can simply take the bishop on c2. If white takes back with the queen black takes the free knight on a6.

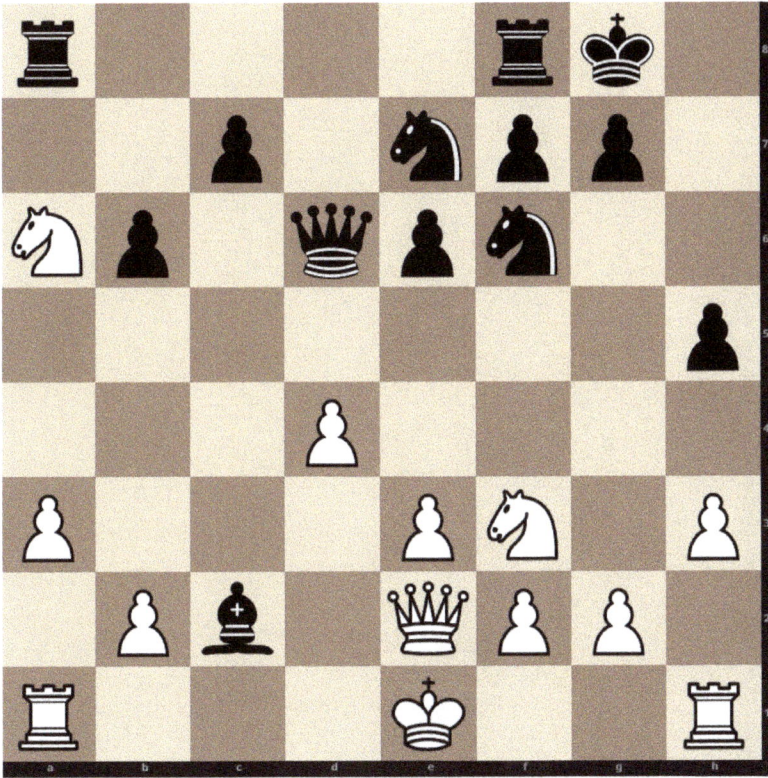

Fig. 15

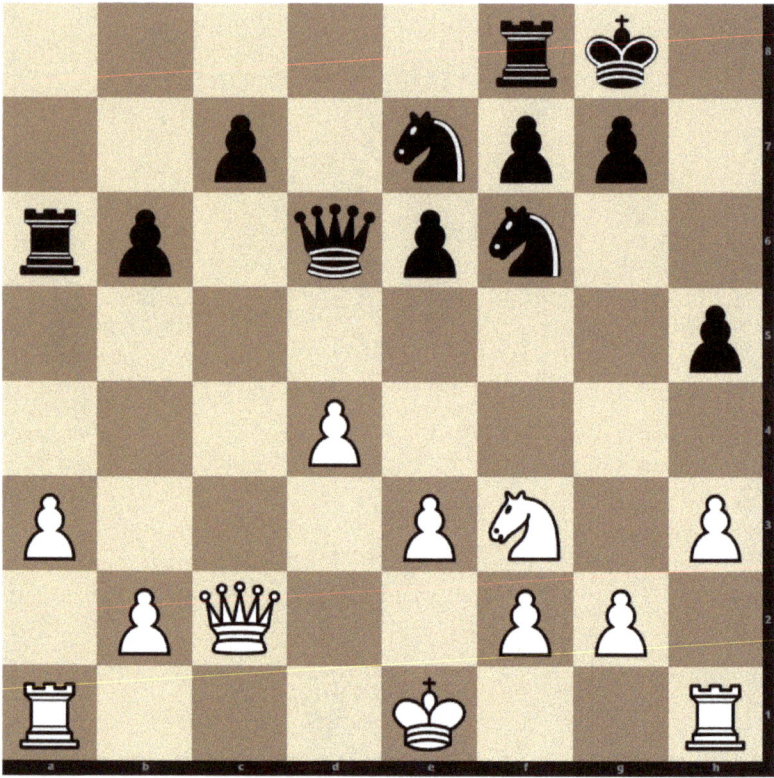

Fig. 16

After position #15 did white have any tricks to save the knight or at least pinch another pawn for it before being captured? How about Nxc7?

Fig. 17

You have to calculate that after Qxc7 which defends the bishop for now, white has Rc1, pinning the bishop to the queen. See position #18.

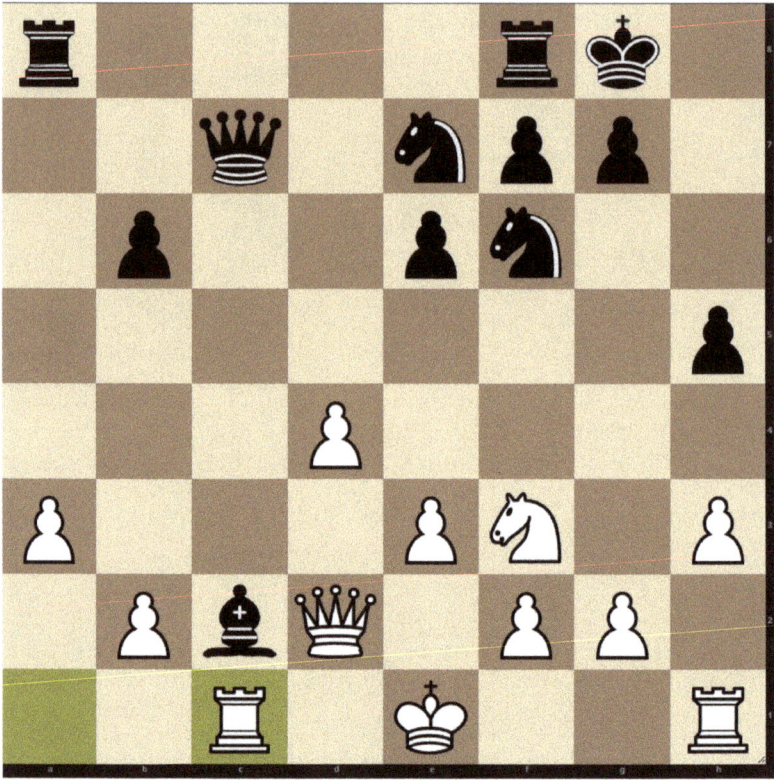

Fig. 18

From position #18, it's likely that black can not defend the bishop on c2 properly and it'll eventually fall when the queen moves out of the pin. However, even when white wins the bishop black has managed to be up a piece for 2 pawns which is better for black.

Fig. 19

Black is already castled, so they decide to move the knight to c4 which centralizes the knight and comes with a tempo on the queen. Queen is forced to take the bishop.

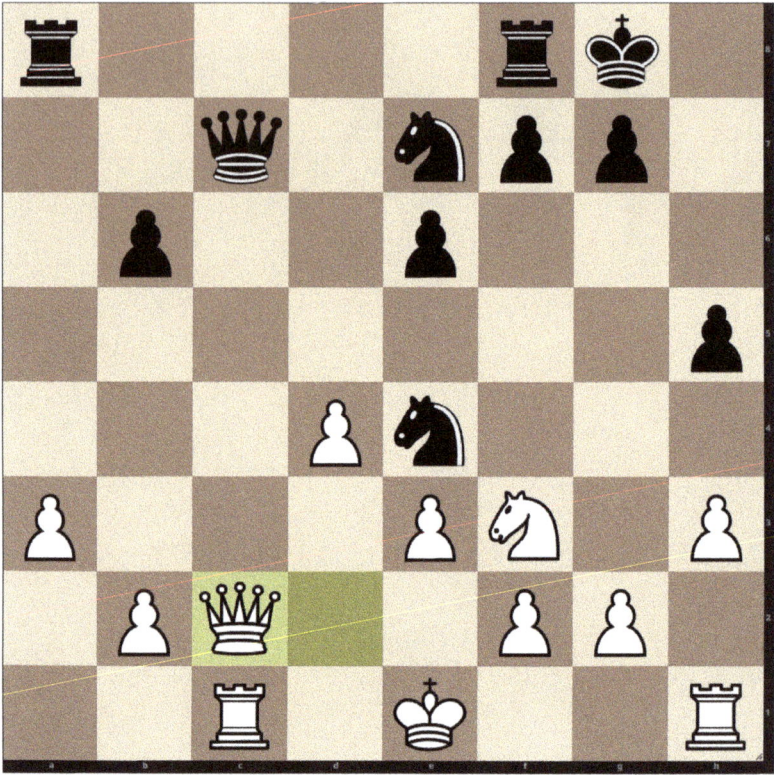

Fig. 20

As black is up material, exchange of queens is in their favor. So they exchange queens on c2. See position #21.

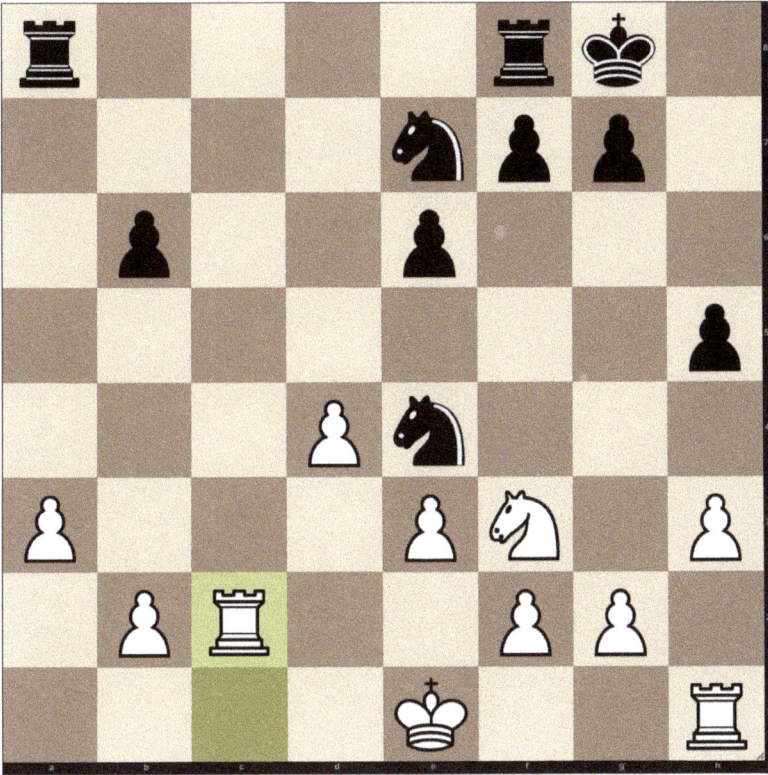

Fig. 21

You might think that this move leaves the control of the c file to white, but it's actually black who has the upper hand in this position. They have a central knight on c4 and can contest the c file by moving one of their rooks to the c file. See position #22.

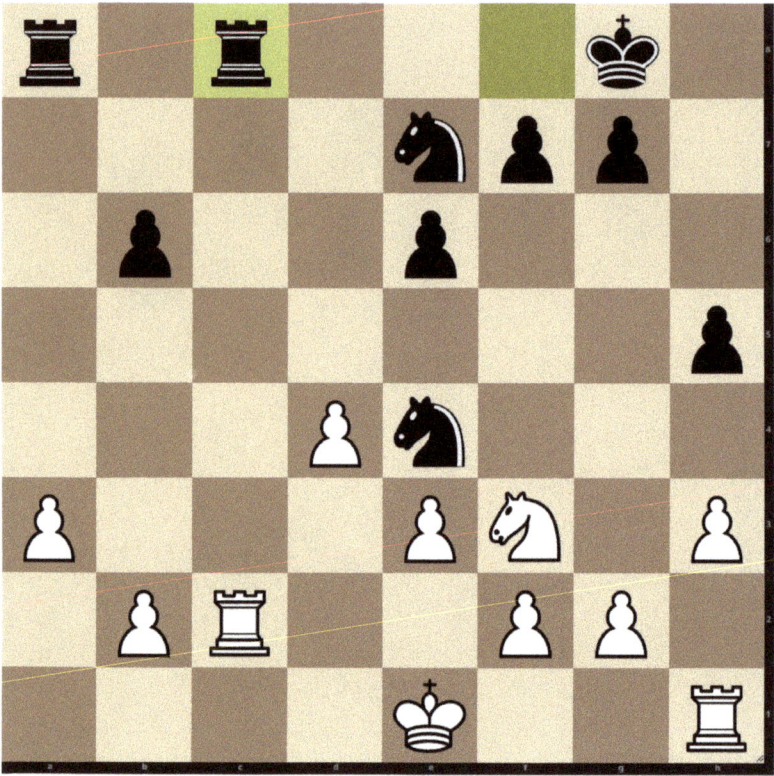

Fig. 22

Black decides to move the f rook to c file, offering an exchange of rooks. White can not ignore this because they have an uncastled king and unable to double rooks on the c file retaining control of the file with a rook. Rooks are stronger on open files. White is in a bad situation because exchanging the rook and getting closer to an end game is not in their favor. Here white is forced to exchange the rook. Note that white can not decline the exchange and go Re2 to save the rook because black's next move will be checkmate Rc1#.

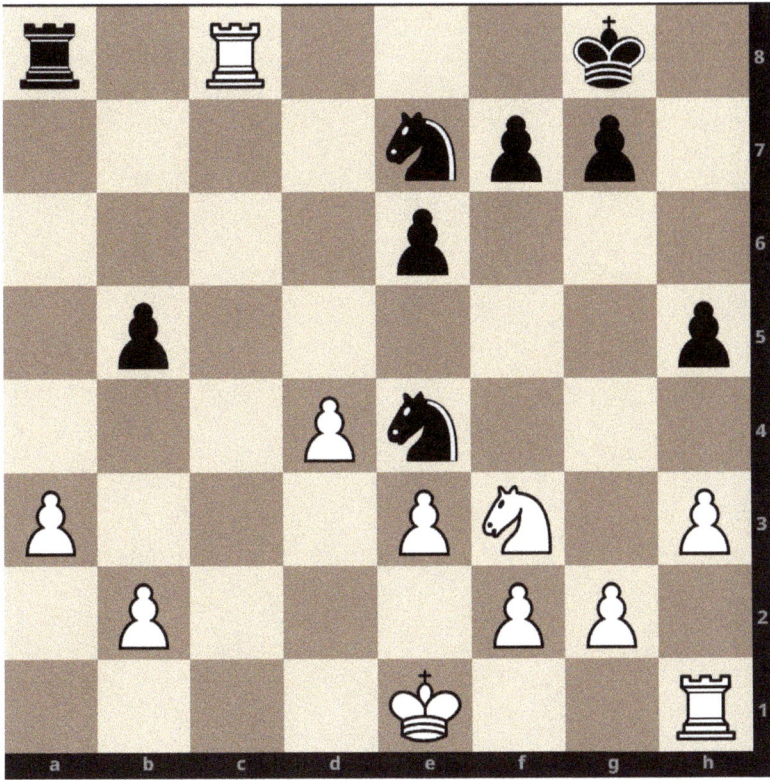

Fig. 23

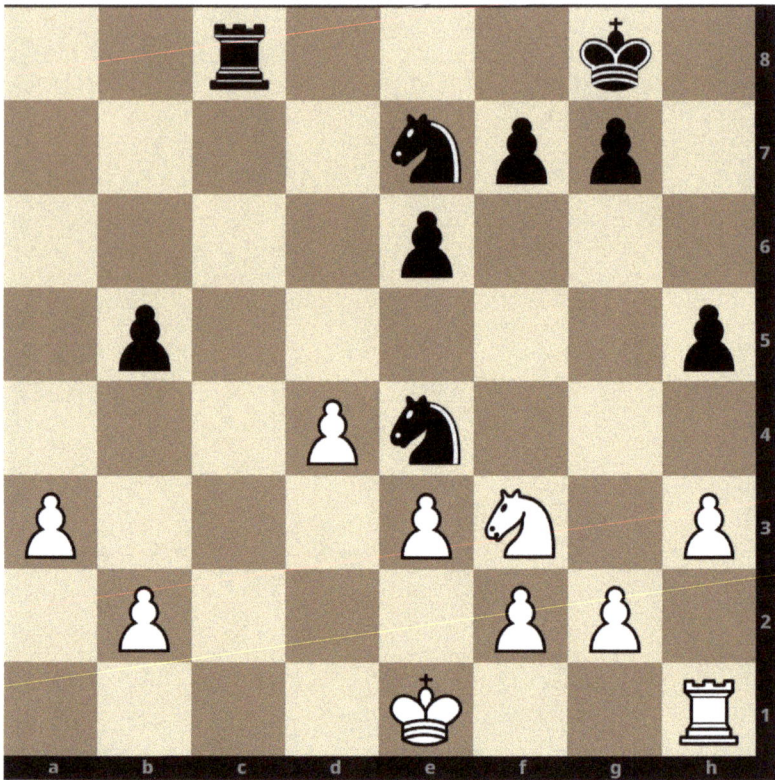

Fig. 24

Black is clearly better: They are up material and they have control of the only open file on the board with their rook. Black has an active check threat on c1 which can only be parried by moving the king to Kd1 which allows the knight fork with Nf2+. White is losing the rook on h1 either way. If played accurately black should be able to win this game.

Note all whites' troubles came from lack of tactical awareness in position #11. They miscalculated the line and didn't see the bishop threat which overloads the queen in defending both the knight on a6 and bishop on c2. White should have never played a greedy move to pinch a pawn, especially when their king is not castled. After position #11, white must have calculated all this and retreated the knight to Nb3.

5. It's all about the position on the board and not material. Try to solve below puzzle with black to move and win. Consider all moves, even the crazy looking ones.

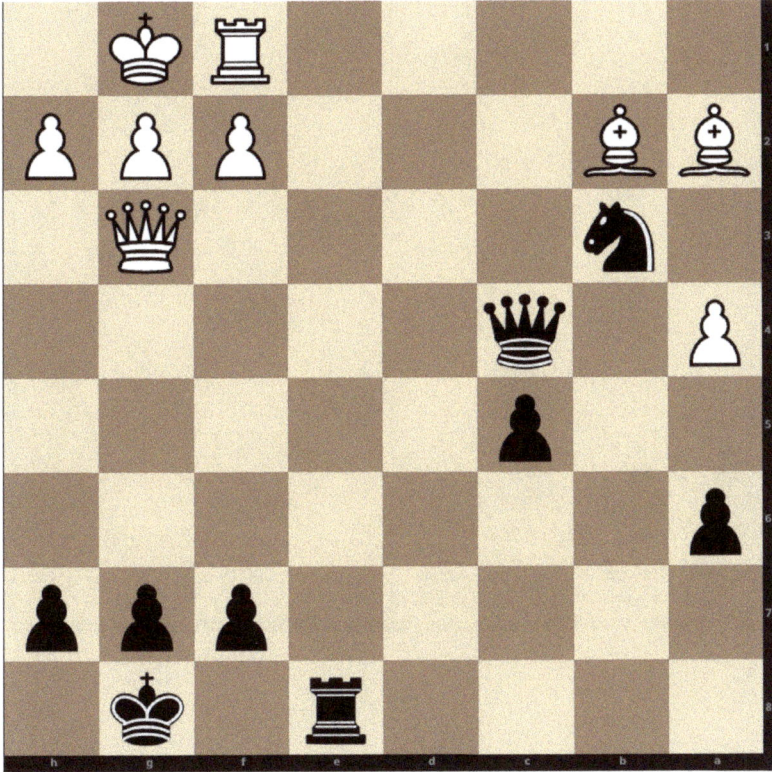

Fig. 25

In this position, black is down a piece and their remaining piece(knight on b3) is pinned to the queen. But if the position dictates that they have a forcing line that checkmate the white king, they are victorious.

You normally don't want to lose your queen(9 points) for rook(5 points) but considering the back-rank weakness of the white king and the fact that rook on e1 does a brilliant job of disallowing white king to come out of back-rank, it's a mate in 3 puzzle. In this setup white can capture the rook on f1 with their queen which comes with check: Qf1+.

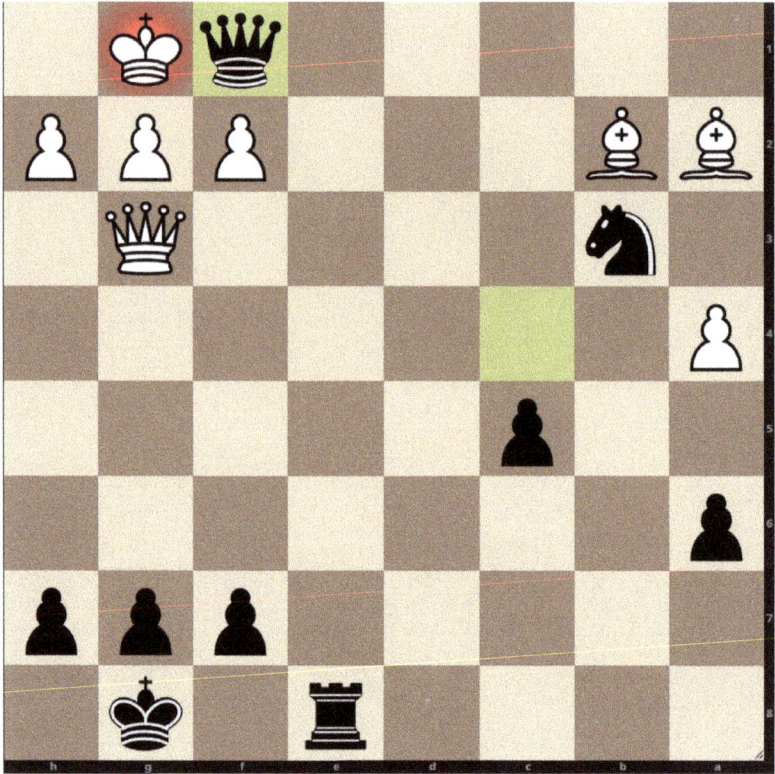

Fig. 26

White king is forced to take back with the king.

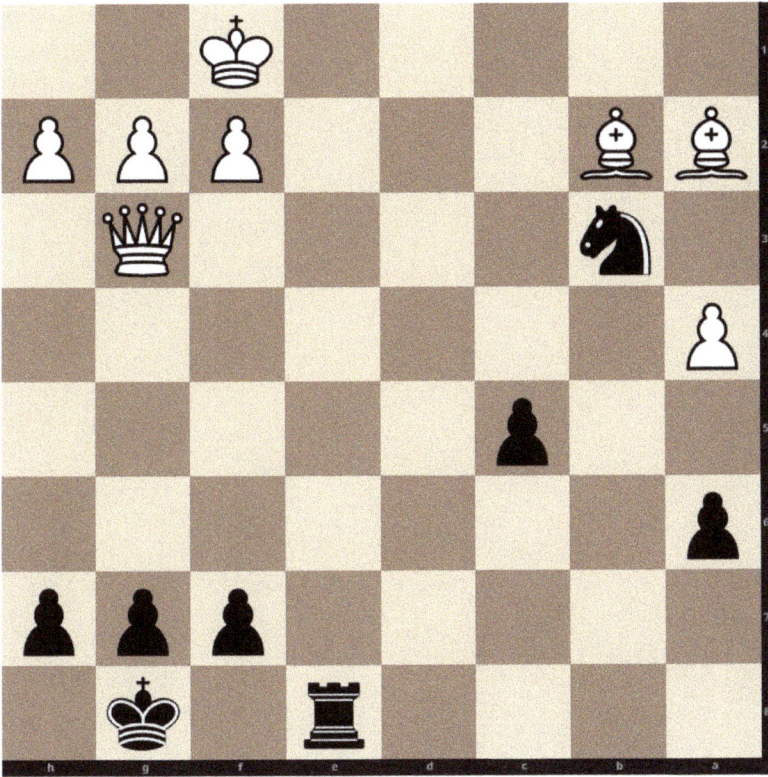

Fig. 27

Now the knight jumps to d2+, delivering a check pushing the king back into back-rank.

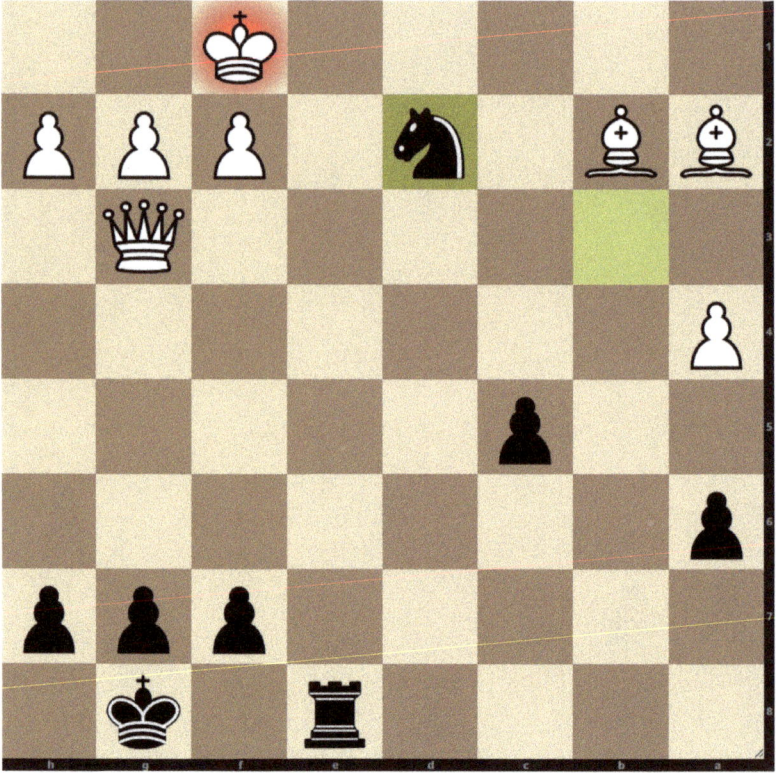

Fig. 28

King is forced to go back to Kg2 which then the rook can deliver checkmate on e1#.

Fig. 29

The queen sacrificed herself for checkmate. Material advantage is of no use for white, if they get checkmated first.

6. Black has misplayed the opening and their king is caught in the middle of the board and they have lost castling rights because the king has moved from his original position. In this position white played Bg5 pinning the knight to the king.

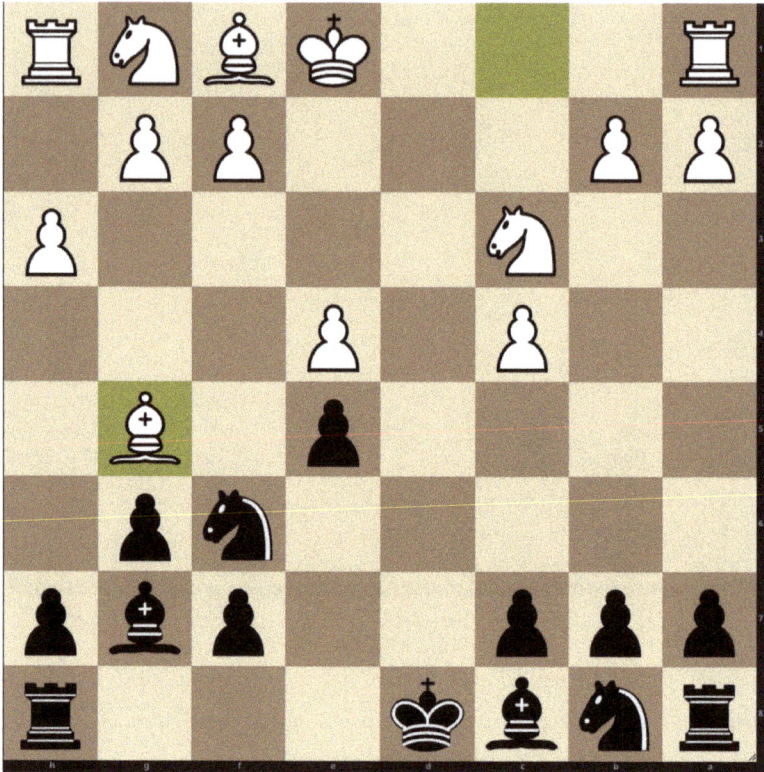

Fig. 30

Black has to be extremely careful and predict the next best move for white. White can castle queen side(o-o-o) with check which seems a very good move. They also can go Nd5 centralizing the knight and double attacking the pinned black knight on f6. Which move is better for white? Long castle that comes with a check or Nd5 with double attack? Calculate both lines and evaluate the end position for both. Choose which is preferred for white.

Let's start the calculation with the obvious double attack on the knight on f6. If white plays Nd5, the knight limits the movement of the king so the king can not defend the knight on f6 because white knight covers e7. Does black have any resources to add protection to pinned pieces on f6? Yes! Nd7 which also covers the king from checks along the d file.

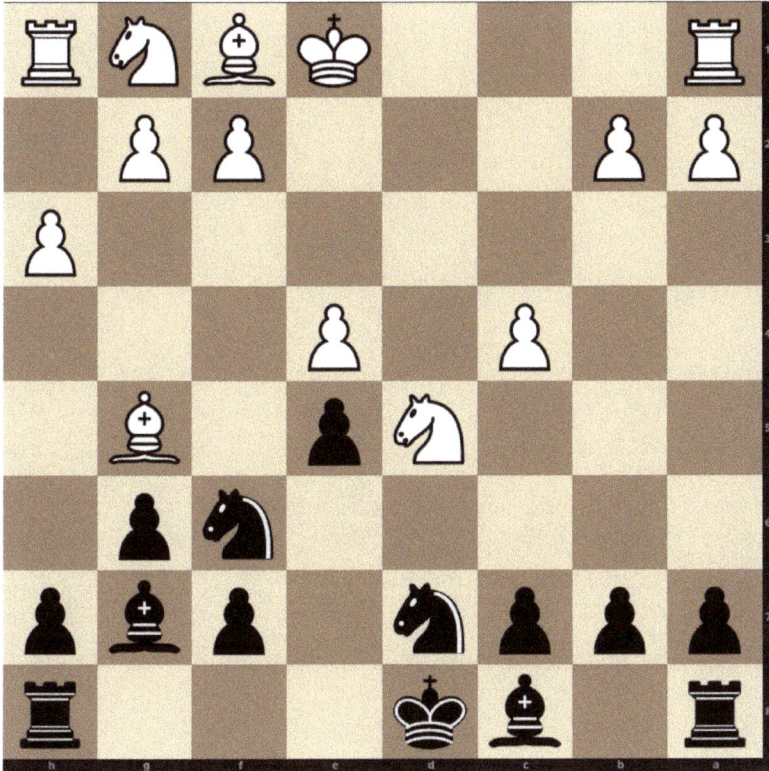

Fig. 31

However, now it's white's turn to play and they see the opportunity to castle long(queen side) which will bring the rook immediately to the open d file pinning the black knight on d7 to the king if the white knight on d5 moves.

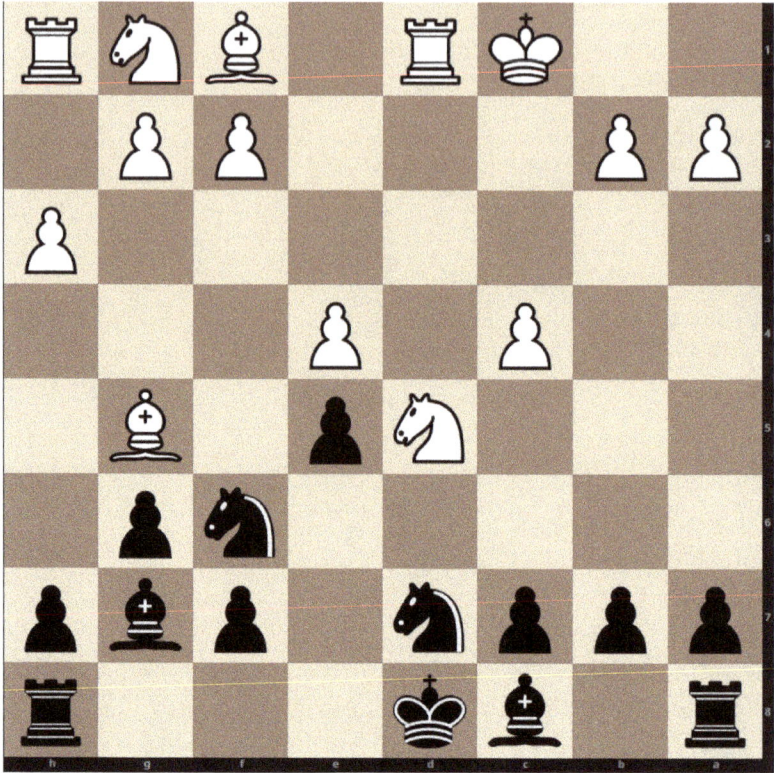

Fig. 32

Let's assume black plays e6 forcing white bishop to take the knight on f6 with a check.

Fig. 33

To not lose more material black chooses to take back with the bishop. And now white takes the bishop for free with their knight.

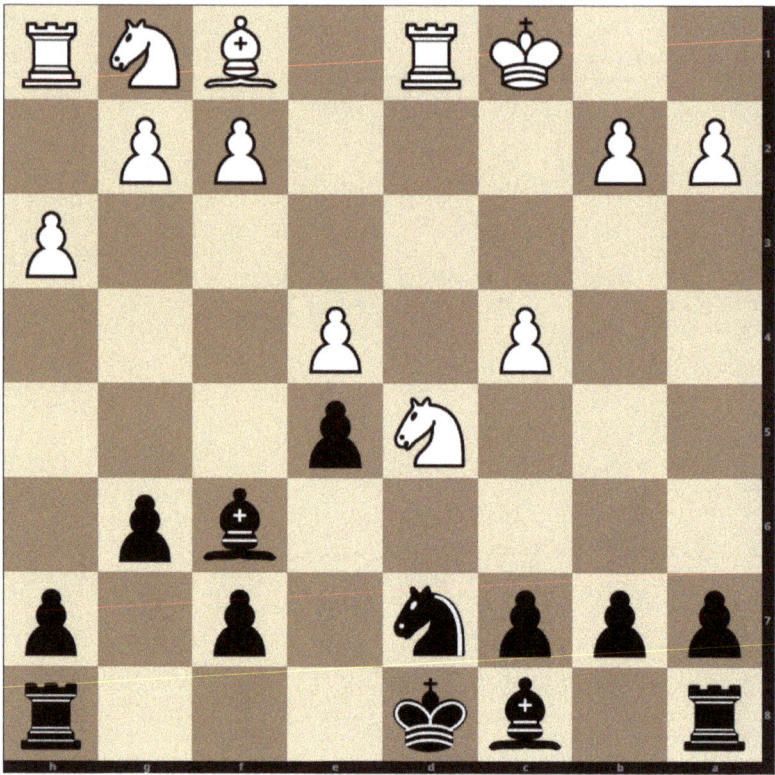

Fig. 34

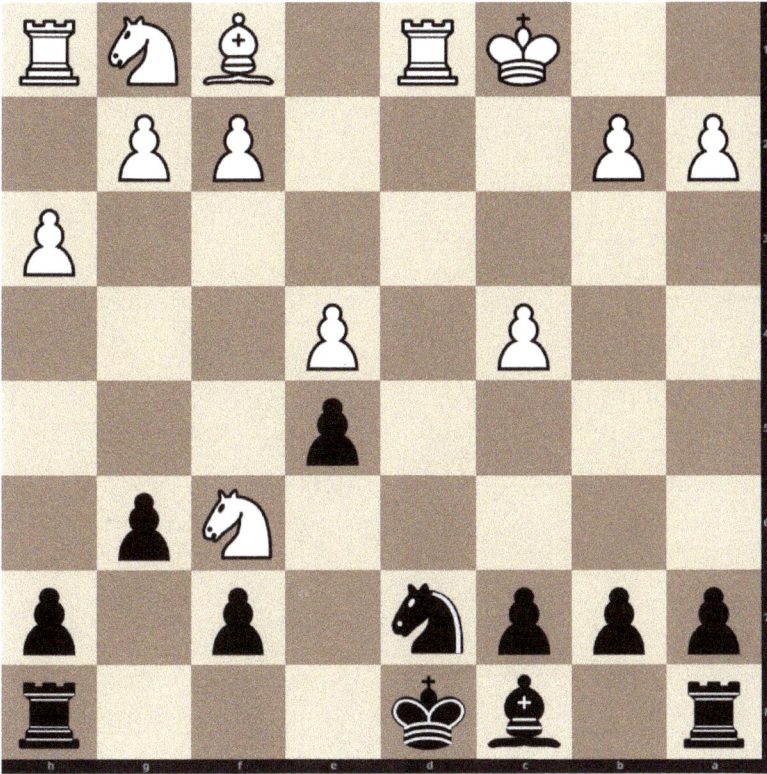

Fig. 35

White takes back with the knight which in turn pins the knight to the king along the d file. White is up a piece(3 points) and will have an easy win. So it's in their favor to continue the exchanges. After black moves, they take the knight on d7.

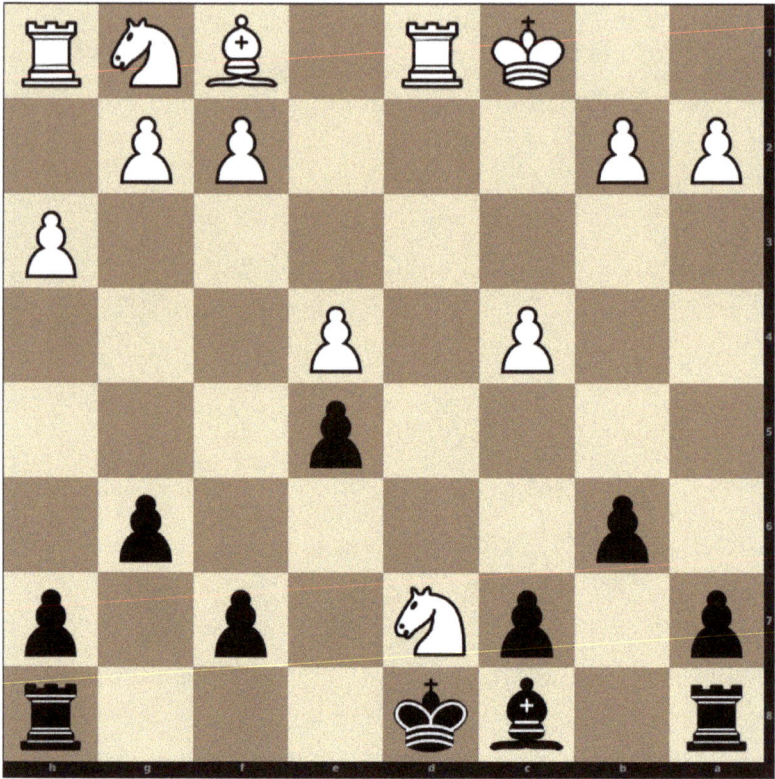

Fig. 36

This forces the bishop to take back and still remain pinned to the king because of the rook on d1. In this line black lost a piece (3 points).

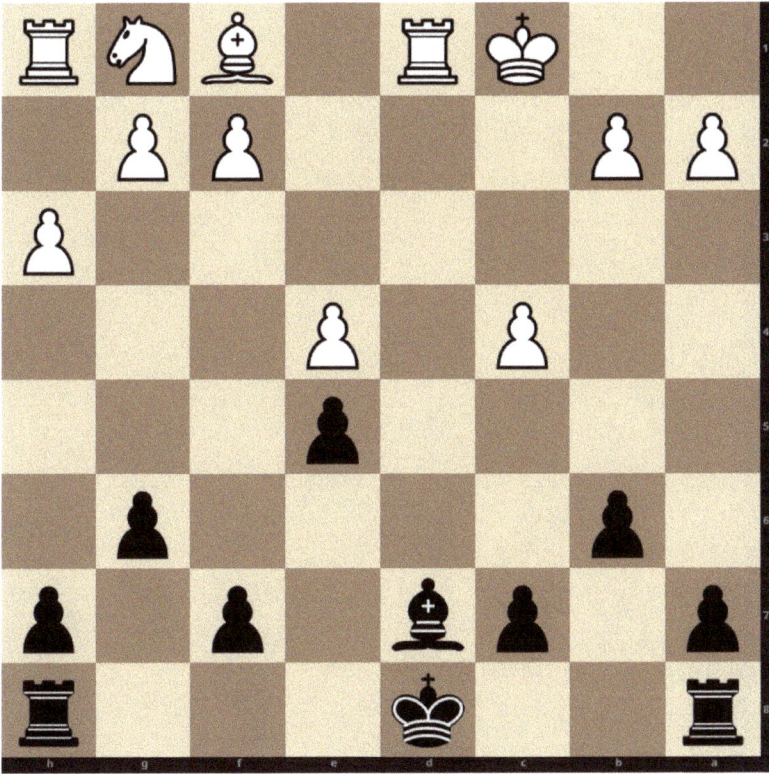

Fig. 37

Now, in position #30, let's calculate the other line starting with the o-o-o (queen side castle) that comes with check.

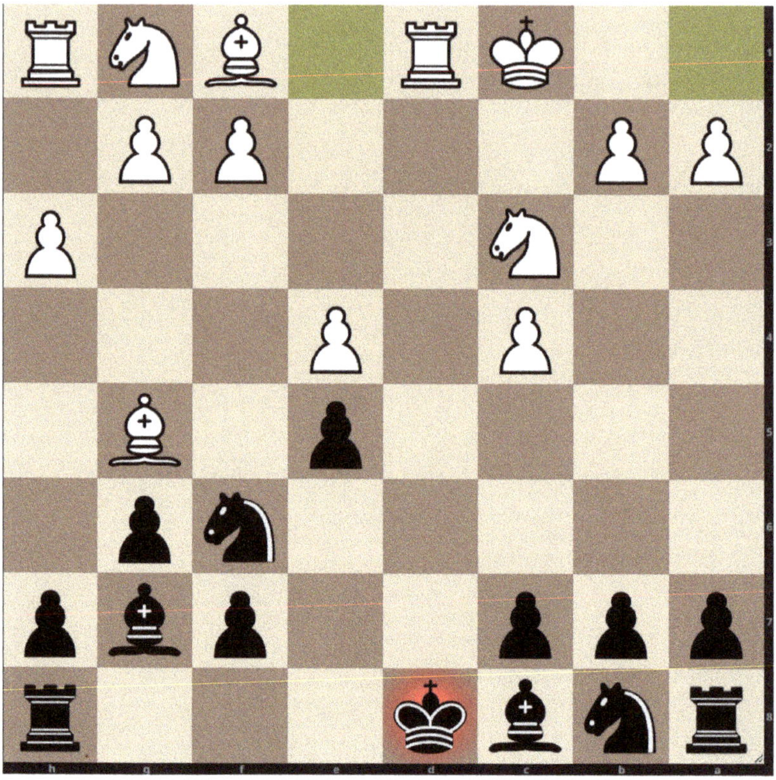

Fig. 38

King can go to e8 or e7 or can block the check with the bishop or the b8 knight. Considering that the next white move will be Nd5 double attacking the pinned knight on f6, king seems to be better off to go to e7 so when the Nd5+ lands he can go to e6 to still support the knight on f6. But this walks into Nxc7+ which forks the king and the rook on a8. This is a good example of good piece coordination for white. White bishop and knight work very well together.

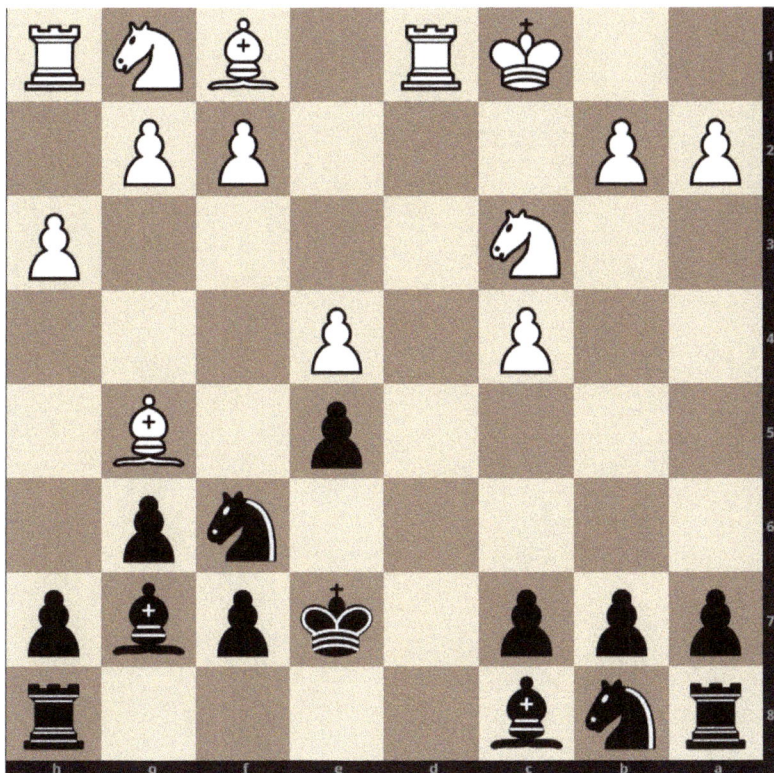

Fig. 39

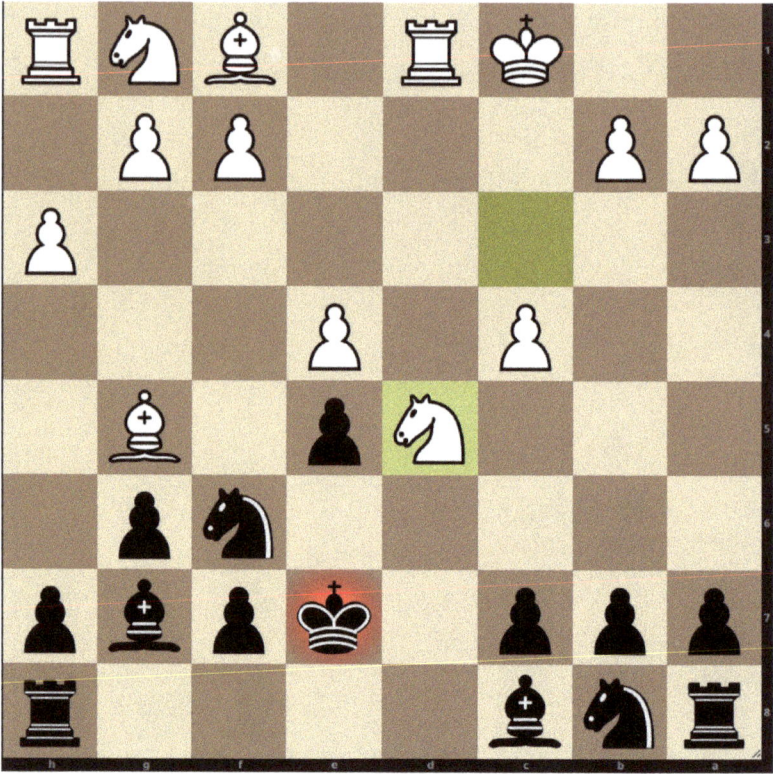

Fig. 40

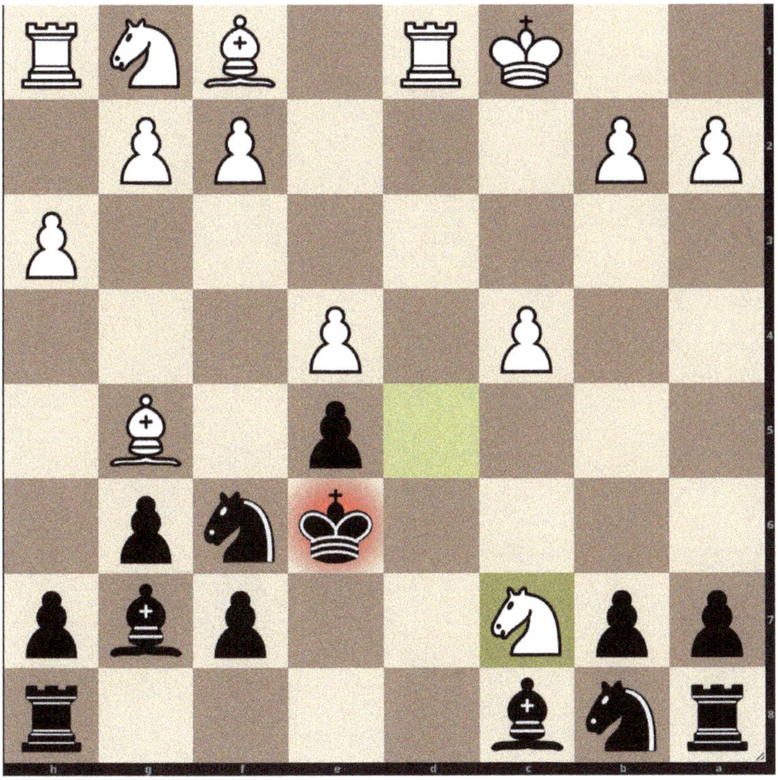

Fig. 41

So this line is out of the question. It's better for black to block the check with the knight (see position #32) and lose a piece instead of a rook. Black should continue playing with a piece down.

If white plays accurately, they should be able to win this game. Because of material advantage it's in white's favor to simplify the position with further exchanges and reducing the chances for black to counter attack.

7.   Below is an example of an opening that went very well for white.

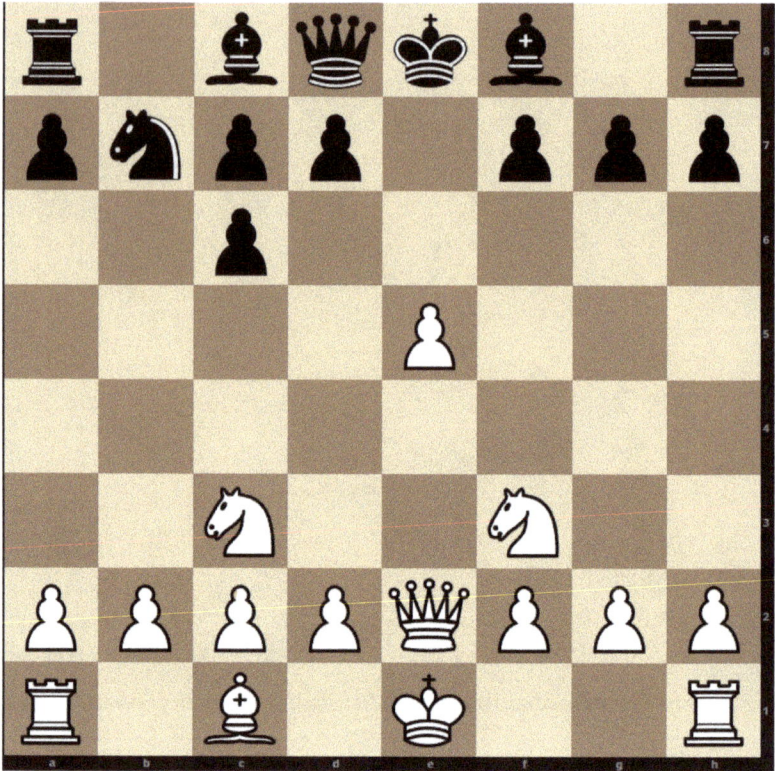

Fig. 42

White has a pawn in the center and black has nothing in the central squares. Both white knights are developed into meaningful squares which control the central squares. Note that whites' pawn on e5 is pushed into enemy territory, i.e. have been pushed into blacks' half of the board. Ranks 1-4 are white territory and black's territory is ranks 5-8. The white pawn is pushed into black's camp.

Note that white has two knights on the 3rd rank, apart from the protected pawn on e5. Black has nothing on the 5th rank, only one pawn on the 6th rank. The knight on b7 is blocking the light square bishop from developing. All in all a very favorable position for white. You must play the opening in a way that resulting position is similar to this, your pieces occupy and/or control the center and pushing enemy pieces into clumsy squares like the knight on b7. White has a clear advantage out of the opening and if they continue to play well they should be able to convert the central domination into a win.

8. Below is an example of opening that went well for black due to unambitious play by white.

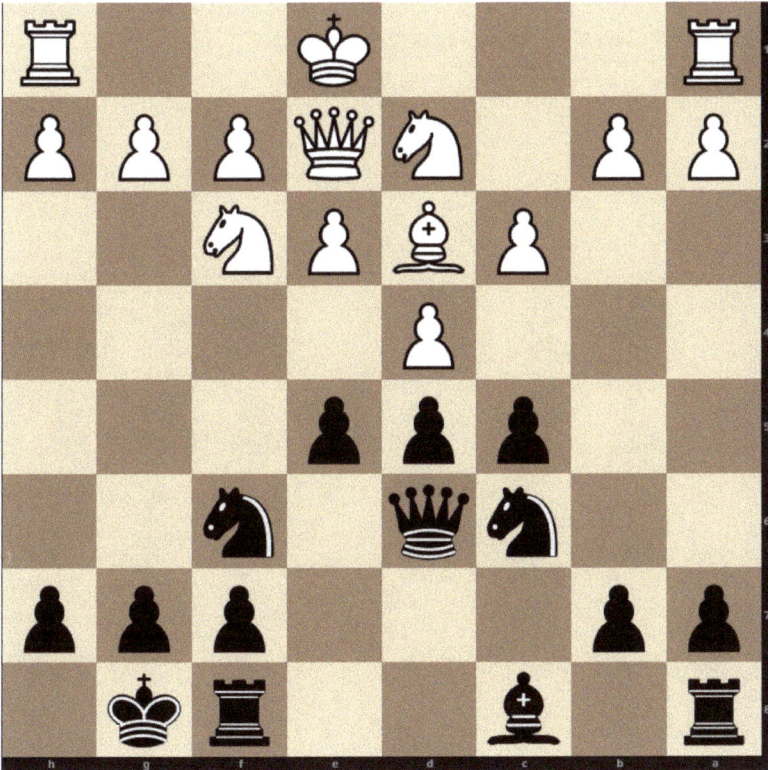

Fig. 43

Black has managed to put two pawns in the central squares e5 and d5, and one pawn in side central square c5 where white has only one pawn in the central squares d4. Black has played the opening very well, already castled where white king is still uncastled. Both black knights are on 6th rank which is more aggressive that whites' setup where they have one of their knights on 2nd rank. The further ahead pieces are, the more aggressive they become. Developing pieces on your 2nd rank is not as aggressive as 3rd rank.

Note that black doesn't release the pawn tensions(cxd4 or exd4) because it still doesn't yield any clear advantage.

White is in danger of a fork and losing a minor piece if they don't react to the pawn on e5. If white ignores this threat and castles, pushing the white pawn to e4 will fork the knight and bishop. White is forced to take the pawn on e4 and force the black to take with their knight which in turn centralizes the knight as well. This is a superior position for black and if played well black should be able to keep the advantage gained in the opening and win the game later on.

9. Another example of central domination by white right after the opening.

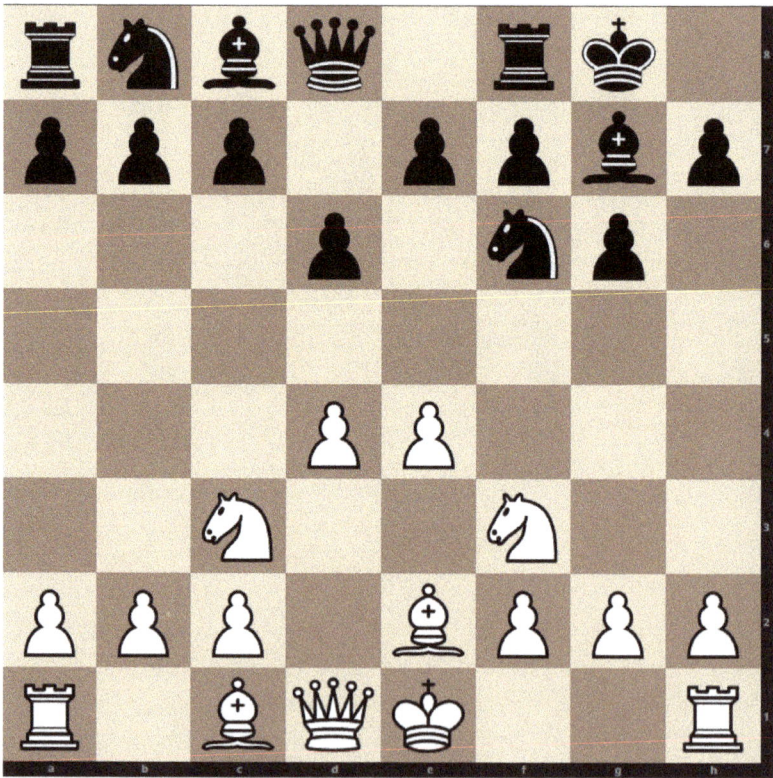

Fig. 44

White has 2 pawns in the center where black has none. White has two knights on the 3rd rank where black has only one knight on 6th rank. Whites' pawns in the center control critical squares in black's camp: c5, d5, e5, f5. Whites' knights add extra protection to e5 and d5 while also controlling b5 and g5.

White has the central domination and if black continues to play passively and do not contest the center soon, they will be behind for the rest of the game. The best play for black in this position is c5 contesting the center from the side.

---

10. In the below example white has managed to put a pawn in the center(e4) where black doesn't have anything in the center. White just played c3 indicating that their next move will be d4. Black has good control over the d4 square for now with the c5 pawn, c6 knight and indirectly with the bishop on g7.

Fig. 45

Considering white has already castled their king but black king is stuck in the middle, black decides to castle and white continues with their plan and plays d4.

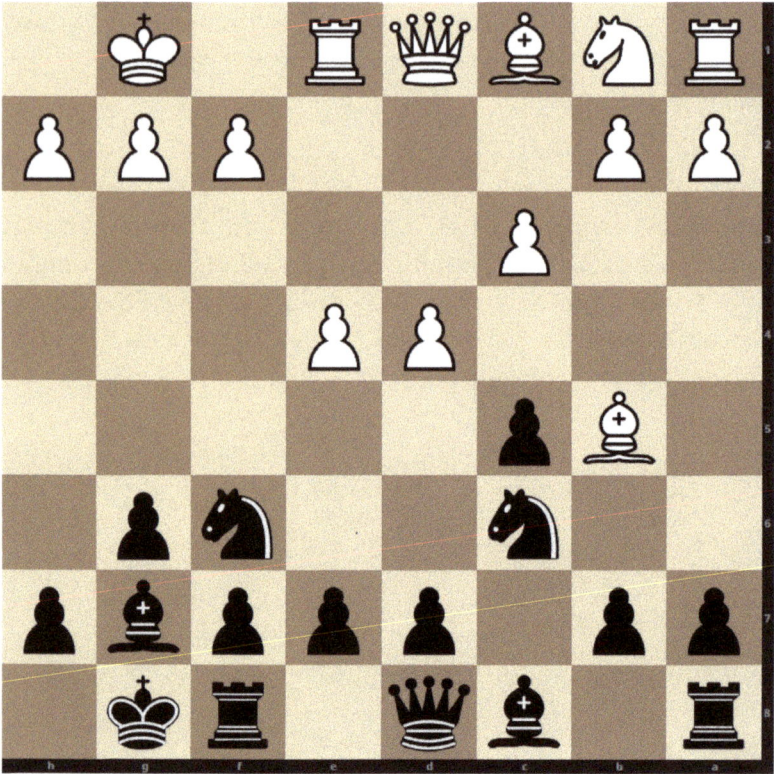

Fig. 46

In this position what is the best move for black? If they decide to take on d4 white will capture back with their c pawn and as a result will retain two pawns in the center as opposed to none by black. cxd4 is a very bad move for black because it will result in more central domination by white. Instead black with their king castled decides to push d5 themself which puts a black pawn in the center (d5). If white captures the pawn with exd5 black recaptures it with knight which centralizes the knight, a brilliant move for black. If white captures the c5 pawn which seems to be free, they just exchange a central pawn (d4) with a side central pawn(c4) which is a bad exchange exchange for white.

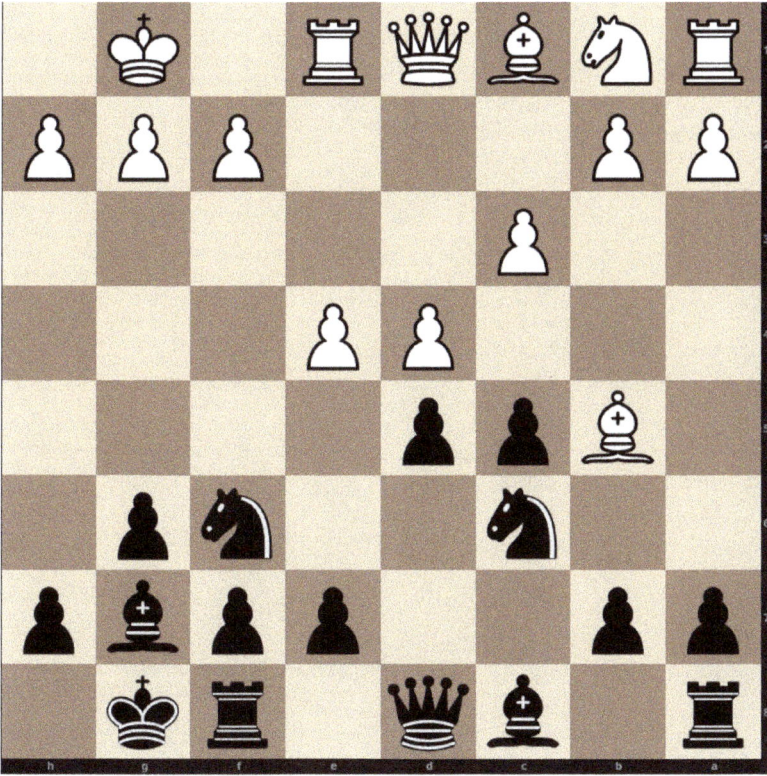

Fig. 47

In this position white is encouraged to push their e pawn to e5 which kicks the knight out which we can use the opportunity to plant that knight in the center(e4). Note that if white pushes the pawn to e5 the extended white pawn on e5 can be harassed later on with pushing the black f pawn to f6.

11. The order of moves is super important. In this example black's last
move is Ra4 offering an exchange of rooks to white. Should white
accept or reject this offer? Does white have a better move in this
position?

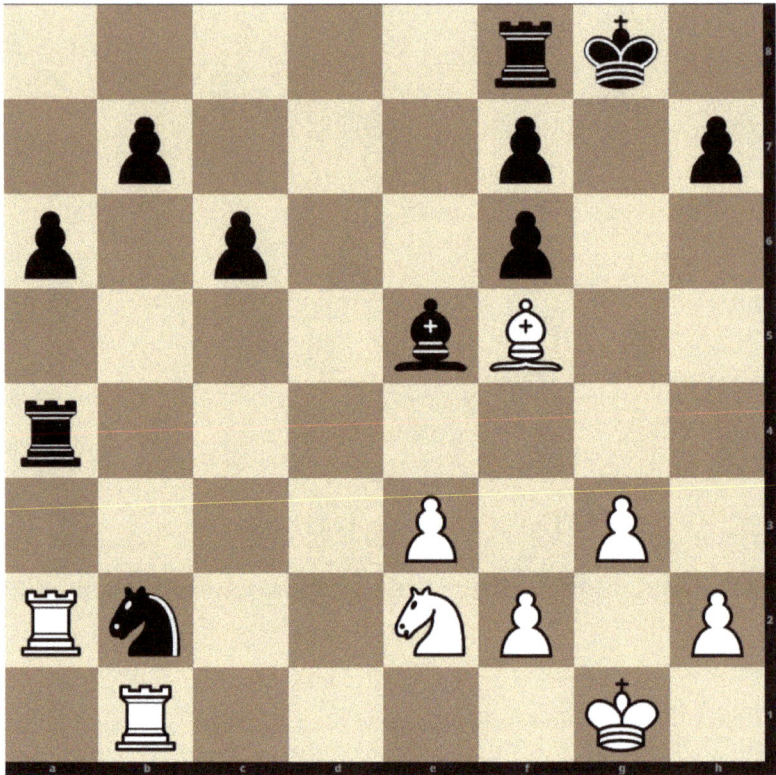

Fig. 48

As you know, two minor pieces are worth more than a rook as a rook
is worth 5 points and each minor piece is worth 3 points. Here white can
take the knight with Raxb2 declining the rook exchange, after black takes
back with Bxb2 white can recapture with Rxb2. Which results in white
taking two active pieces of black for a rook which is a better exchange
for white. This line wins 1 point for white.

What if white takes the knight with the rook on b1? Rbxb2 is a very
good move for white as it removes the defender of black rook. Now
black is forced to Rxa2 which white can recapture with Rxa2. This is the
best sequence of moves for white. In this line white is up a whole piece(3
points), hence this is the best move for white.

The best line for white is Rbxb2 - Rxa2 - Rxa2. In the final position black lost a knight and gained nothing for it, which means white is up material now.

---

12. In the position below it's black to move and win. This is an example of sacrificing on an empty square. When calculating lines always look at checks, captures, threats in this order. Consider all legal moves, regardless of how crazy or suicidal they look.

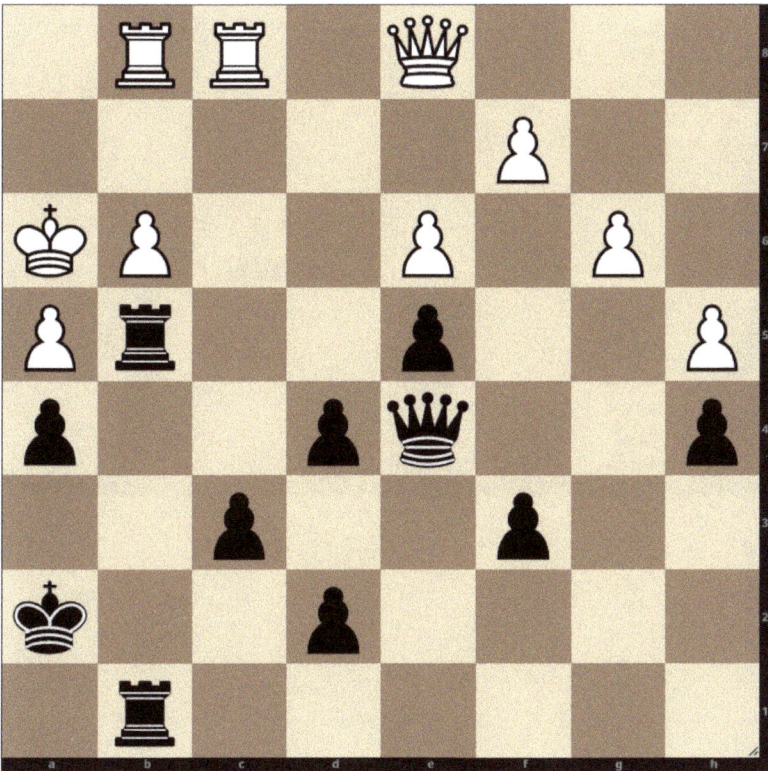

Fig. 49

King is very vulnerable on the b-file, with a check on b6 awaiting if black manages to deflect the defender of the b file: b8 rook. Qa8+ is a brilliant move as it forces Rxa8

Fig. 50

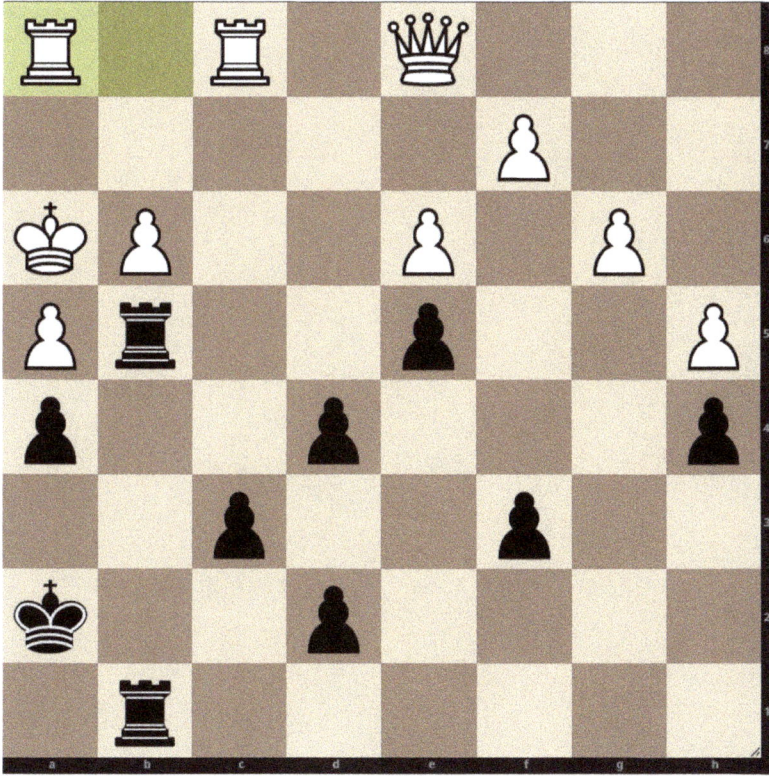

Fig. 51

This is a forcing line with check that deflects the defense of the b-file so the 2 rooks can deliver the checkmate sequence with: Rb6+, Ka7, Rb7+, Ka6, Rb6#.

Fig. 52

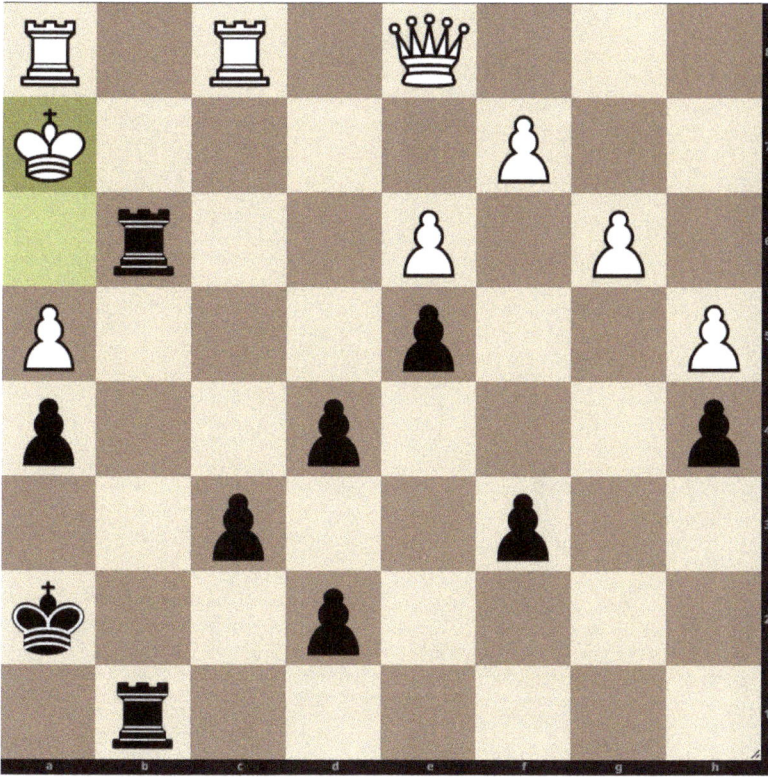

Fig. 53

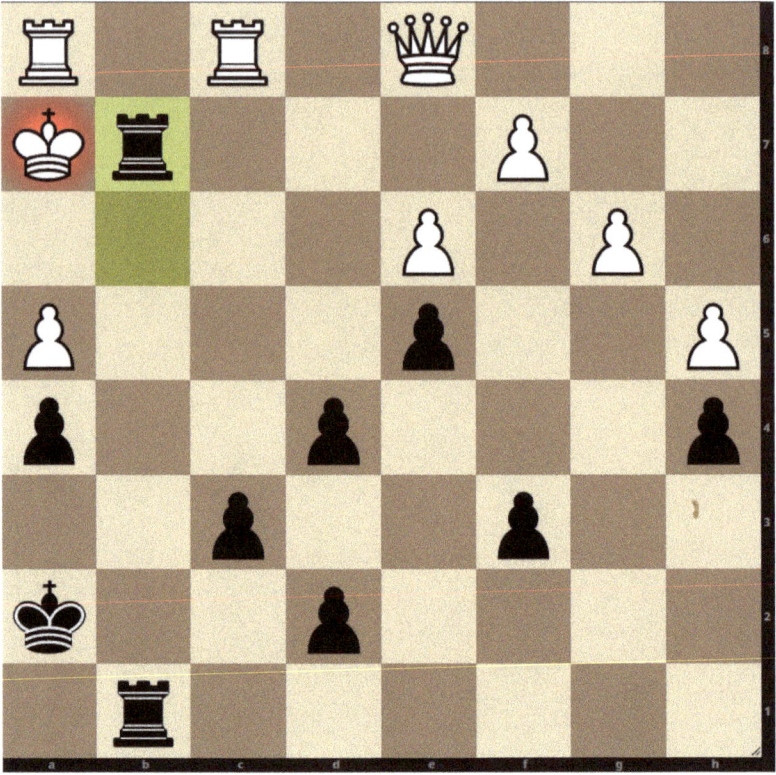

Fig. 54

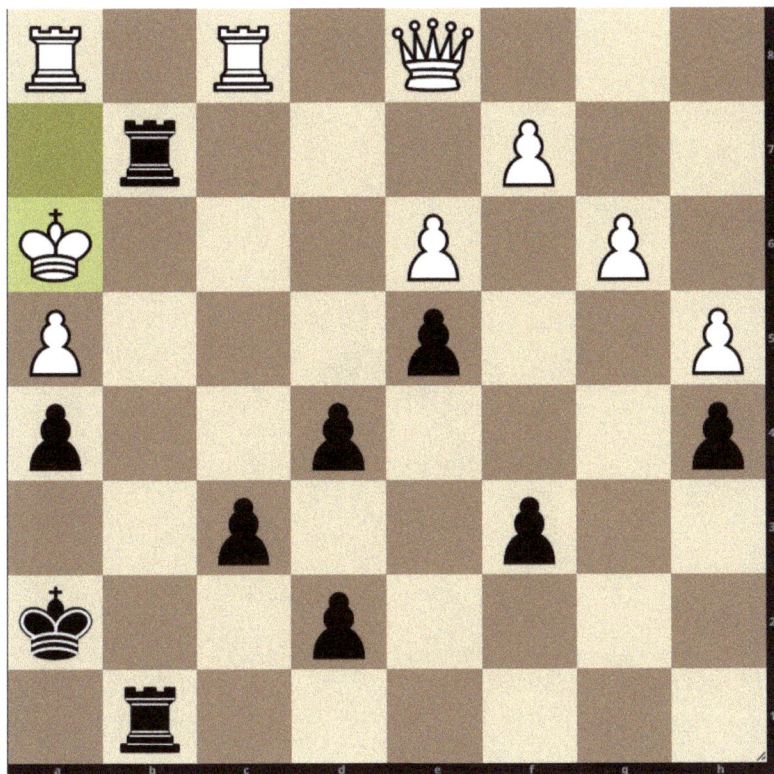

Fig. 55

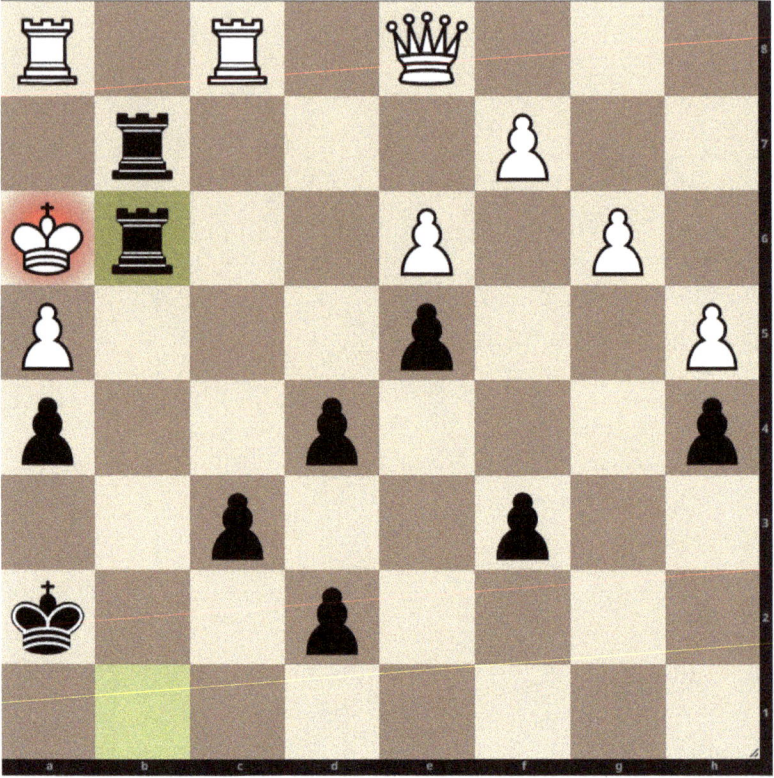

Fig. 56

13. In the position below it's white to move and win. This is an example of sacrificing on an empty square.

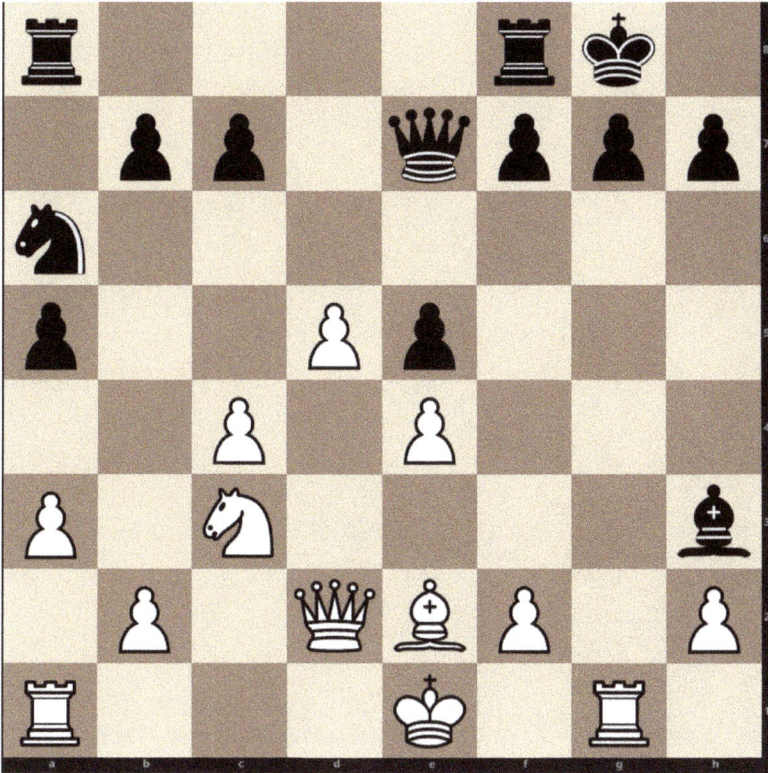

Fig. 57

With Qh6 black is threatened with checkmate on g7

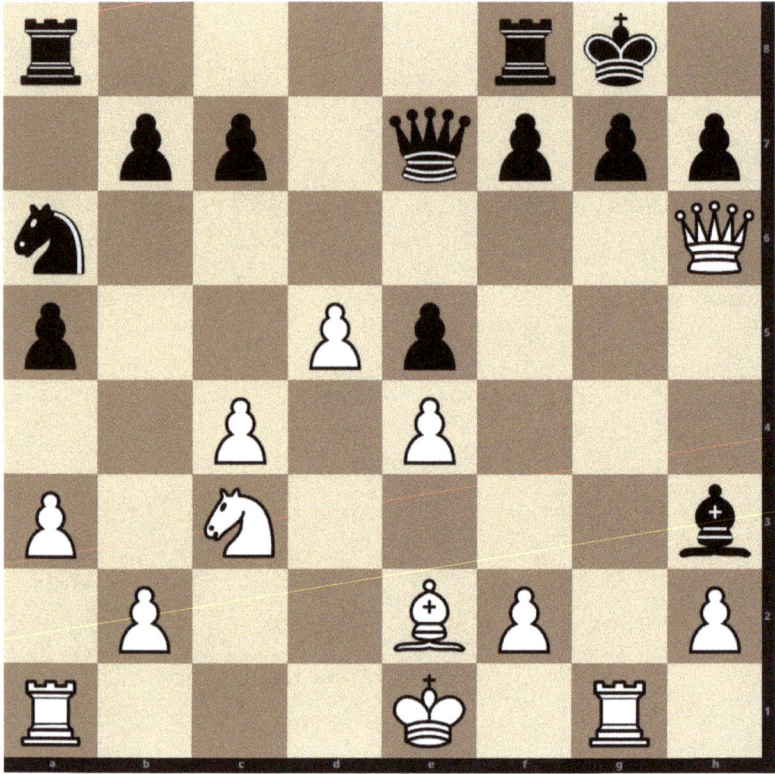

Fig. 58

Black's next move is forced to stop the checkmate, he pushes the pawn: g6

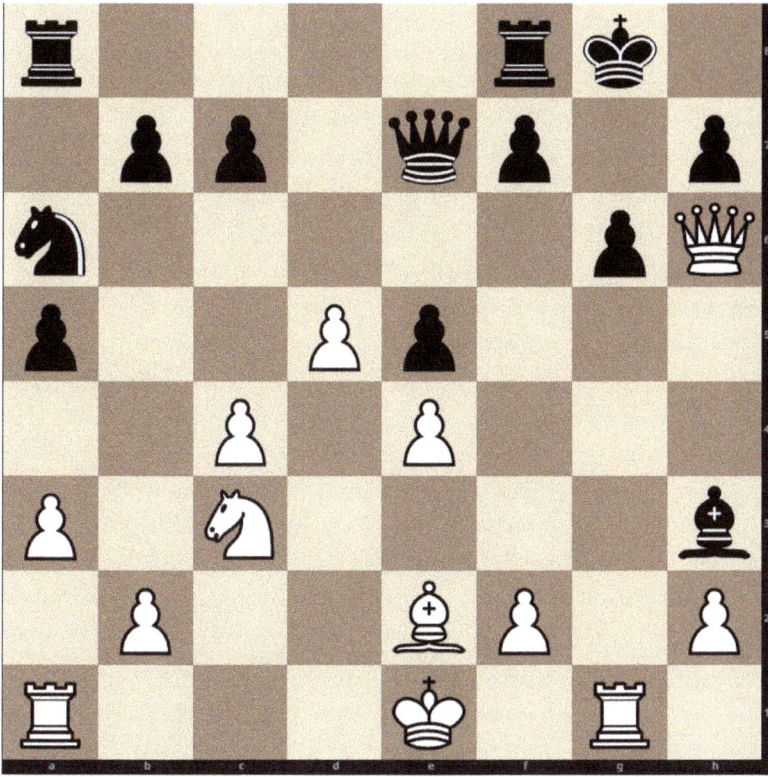

Fig. 59

Now white wins the bishop on h3 for free with: Qxh3

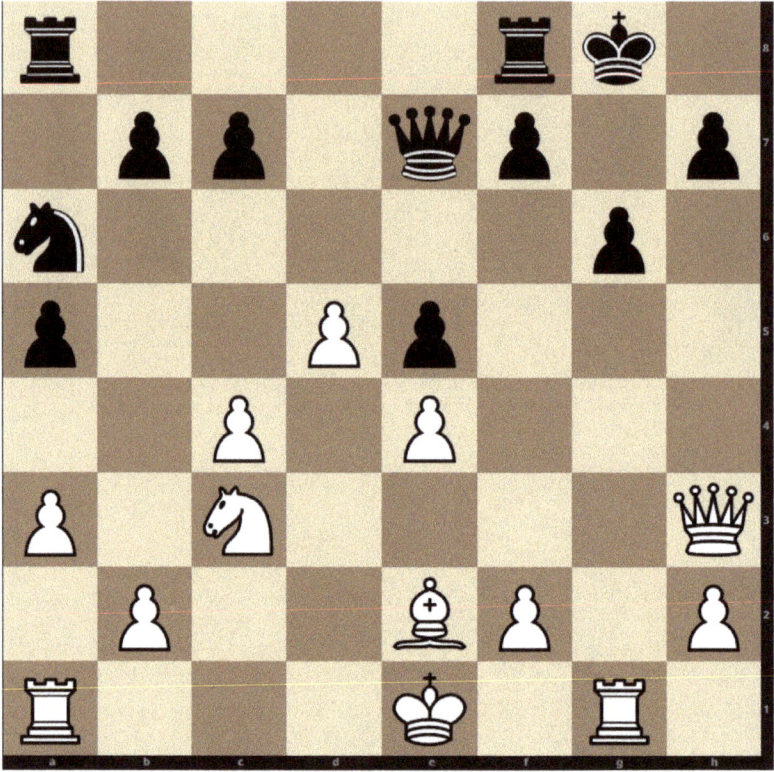

Fig. 60

This position is winning for white with a piece up, better control of the center and a semi-open g file with the rook X-raying the king.

14. In the below position two forcing continuations come to mind: capturing the knight on c6 with knight or queen.

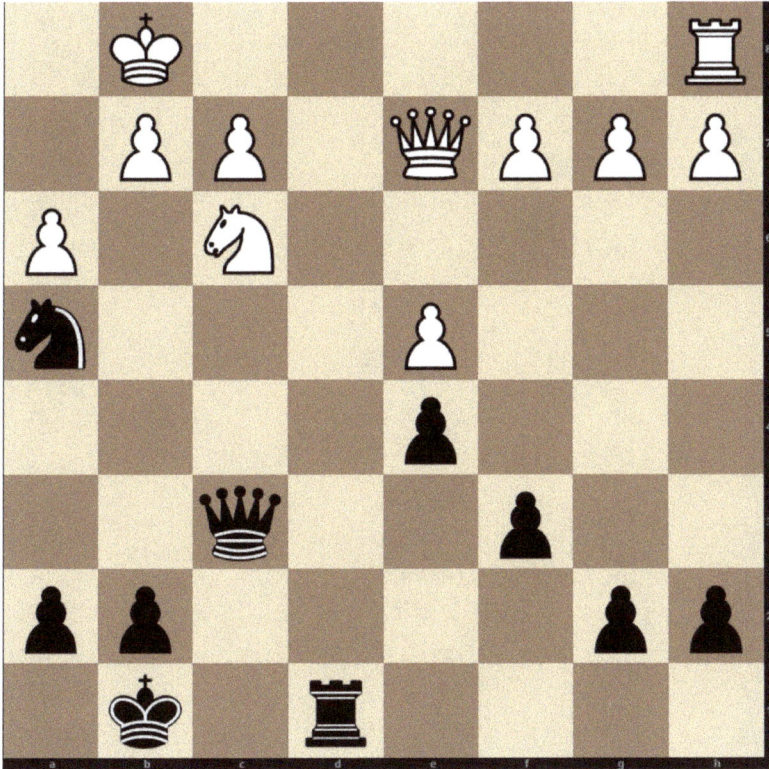

Fig. 61

You have to calculate both and compare the result. 1. Qxc3 bxc3 2. Nxc3+ Ka8 3.Nxe7 wins a piece and gives black an easy end-game.

Taking with knight is a blunder by black because it only wins a pawn where taking with the queen exposes the white king to the awkward fork winning a minor piece in the process.

15. In below position black can take advantage of whites' neglect and win a piece. Black to move:

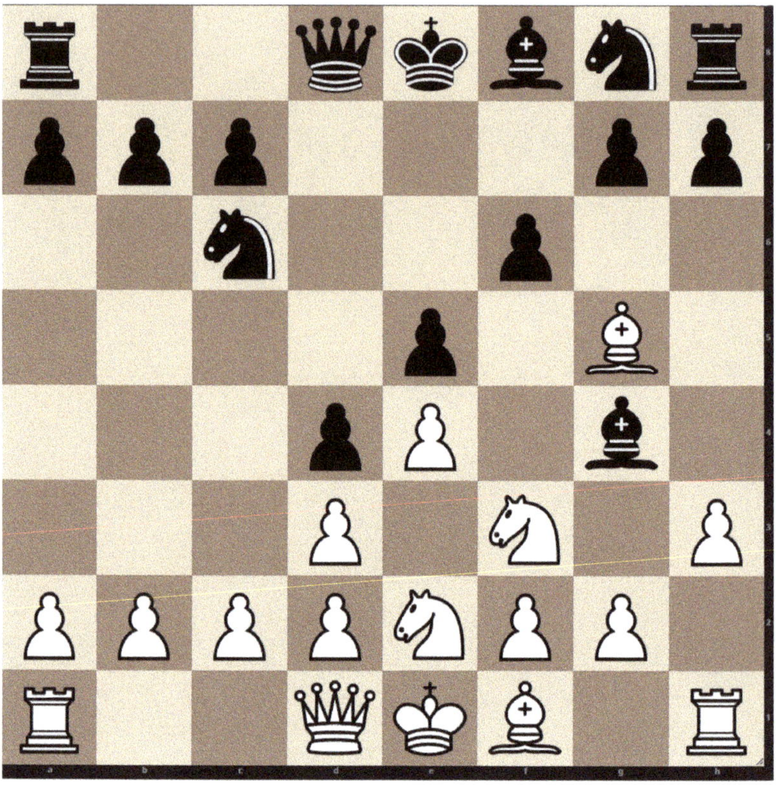

Fig. 62

Black takes the knight on f3 by: Bxf3

Fig. 63

Forcing white to take back with the only option: pawn: gxf3

Fig. 64

Giving black enough time to take the defenseless bishop on g5 for free by: fxg5. This gives black enough material advantage to win the game. Also black has 2 pawns in the center where white only has one and black's pawns are more advanced so it's all an advantageous position for black.

16. In below position: White to move. Do you see the double attack?

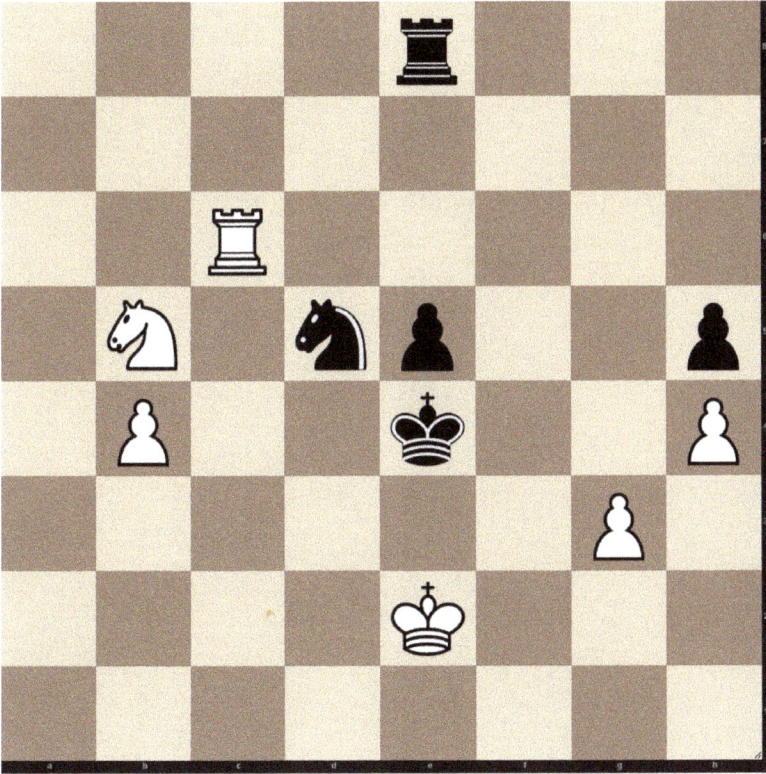

Fig. 65

White has to calculate correctly and see that 1. Nd6+ Kd4 is forced.

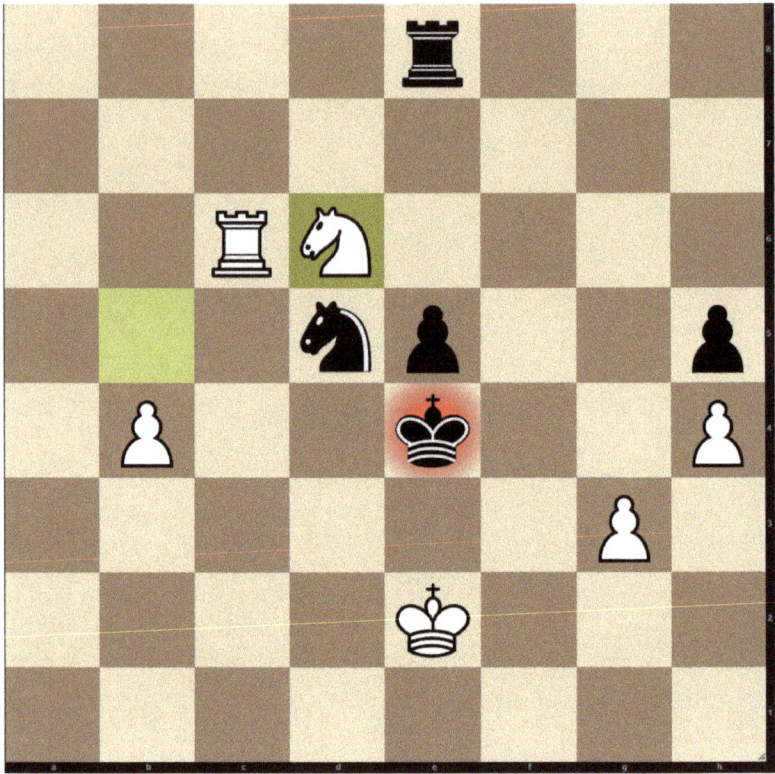

Fig. 66

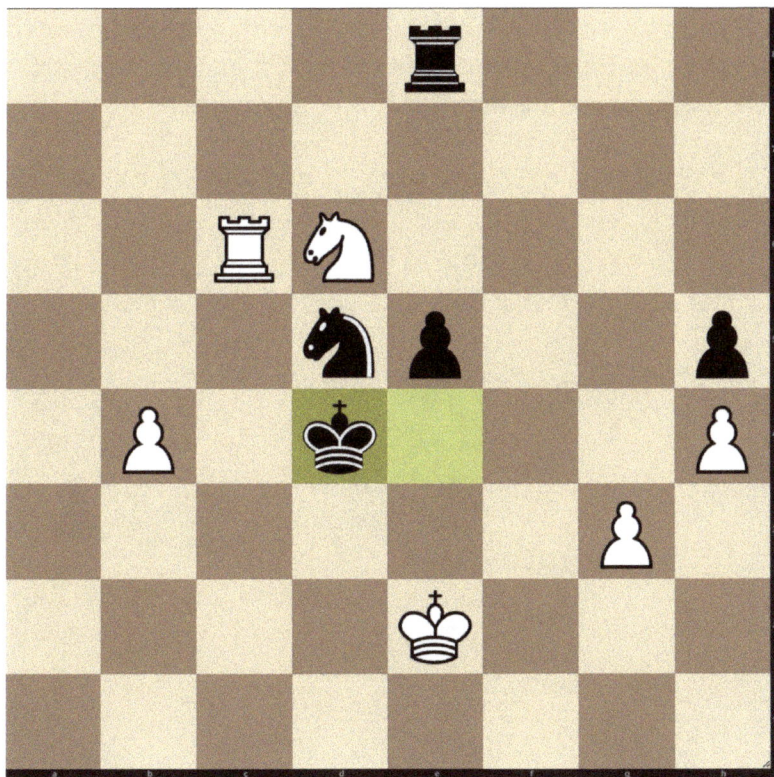

Fig. 67

White has a free rook to capture on e8, but is that the best move for white? Black's king is very vulnerable in the middle of the board with very limited squares to go to. White should not think materialistic, instead need to calculate correctly that Rc4# is checkmate.

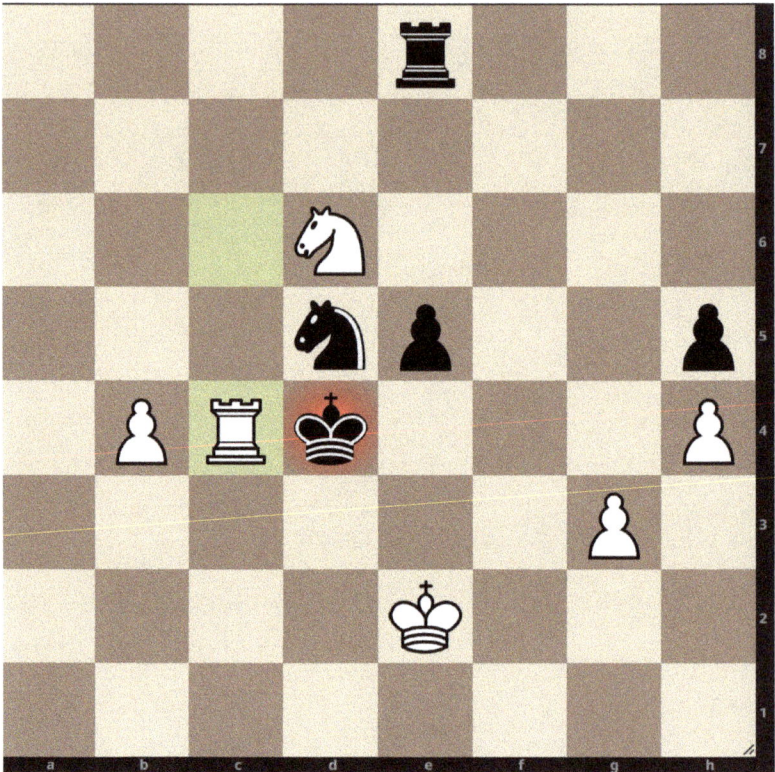

Fig. 68

17. In below position it's black to play. Black has managed to create a battery of rook-queen on the e-file which gives chances to black to play a threatening move.

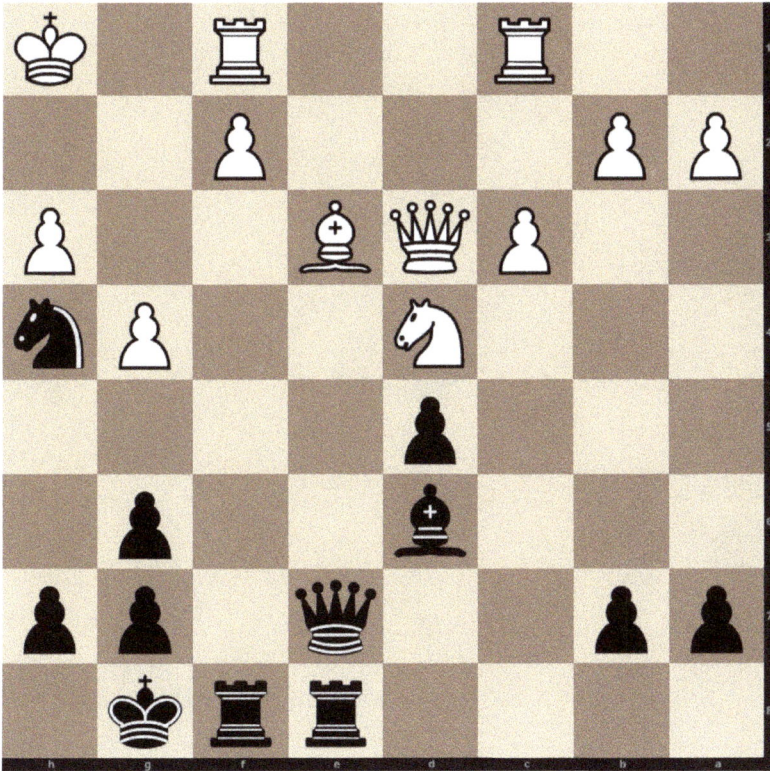

Fig. 69

Black can centralize the queen by Qe5 and threaten check-mate on h2

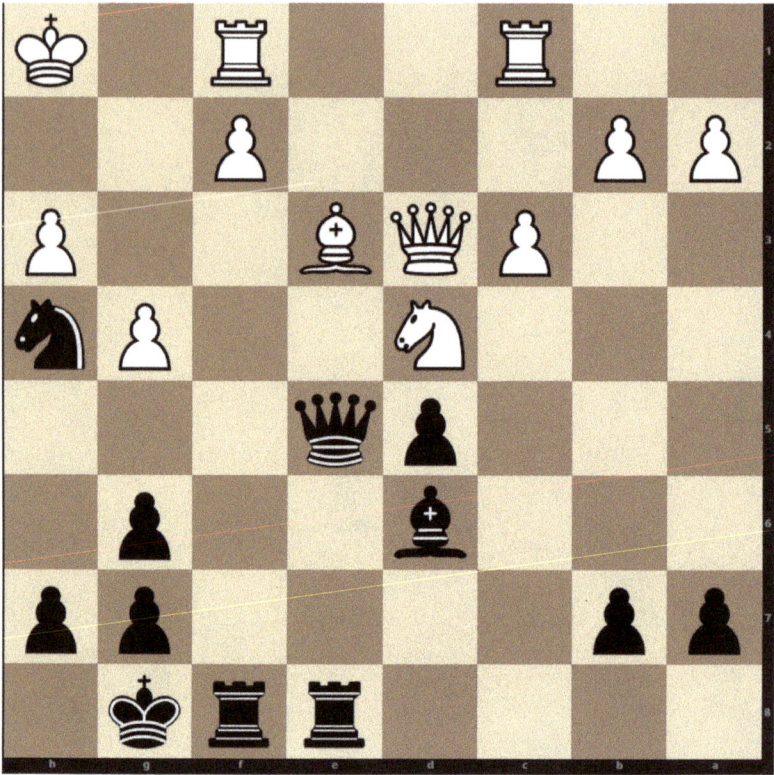

Fig. 70

The only way for white to stop the checkmate threat is to play: f4

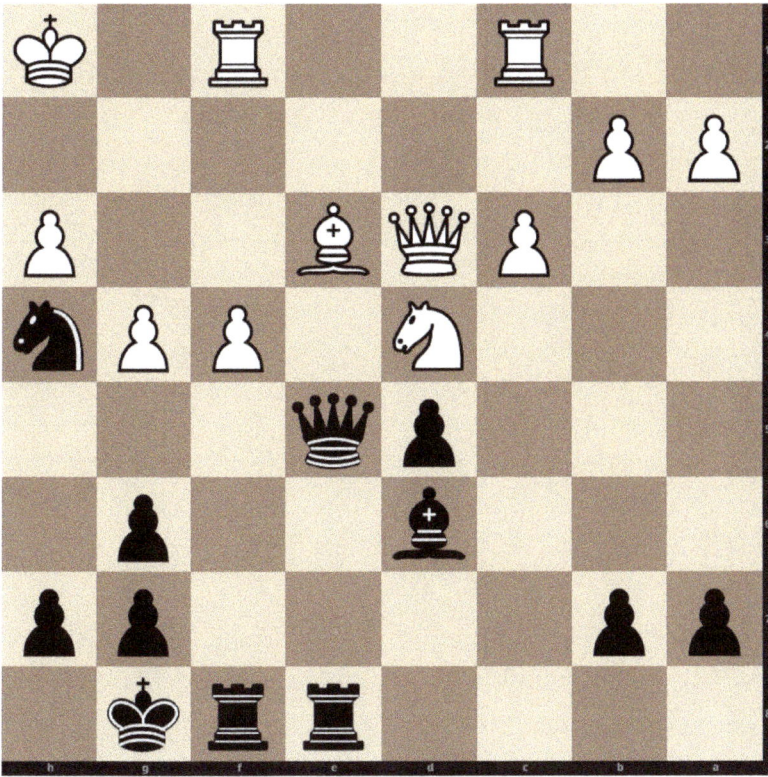

Fig. 71

Which gives black time to capture the defenseless bishop for free by: Qxe3 which in turn will give black the upper hand to win an easy end-game.

18. In the below position, it's black to play. Instead of an automatic re-
take on c4 black needs to think about the next white move which is
obviously taking the defenseless bishop on d4 for free. Black can
stop this with a check, before taking back the queen.

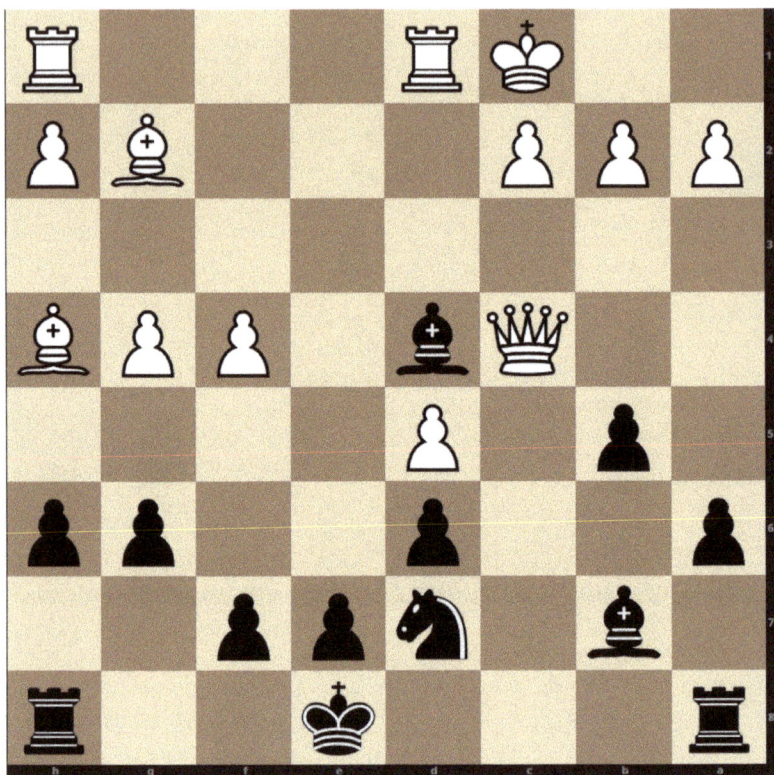

Fig. 72

Fig. 73

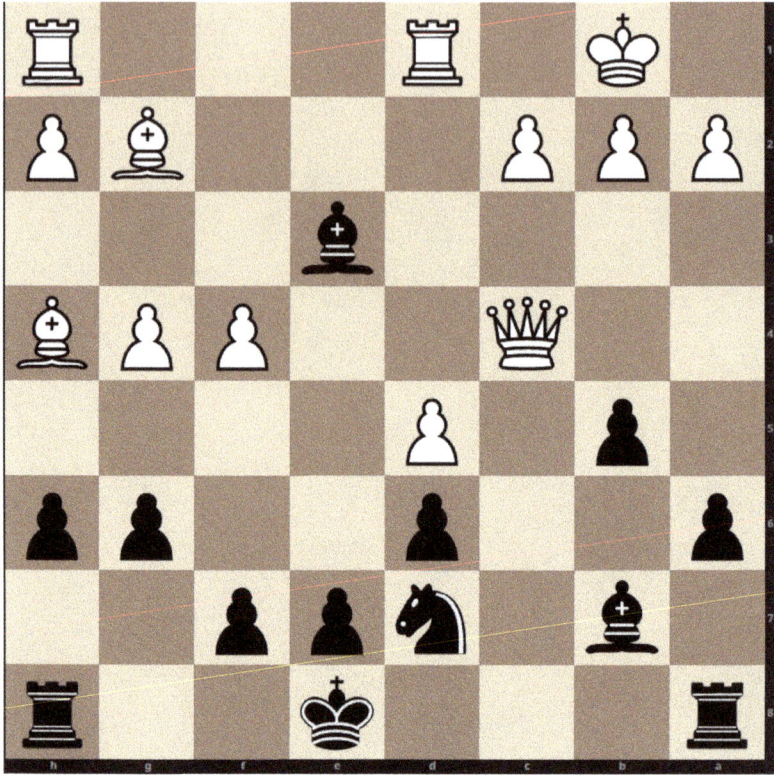

Fig. 74

This sequence of checking first and then retaking the queen saves black's dark square bishop and eventually wins the game.

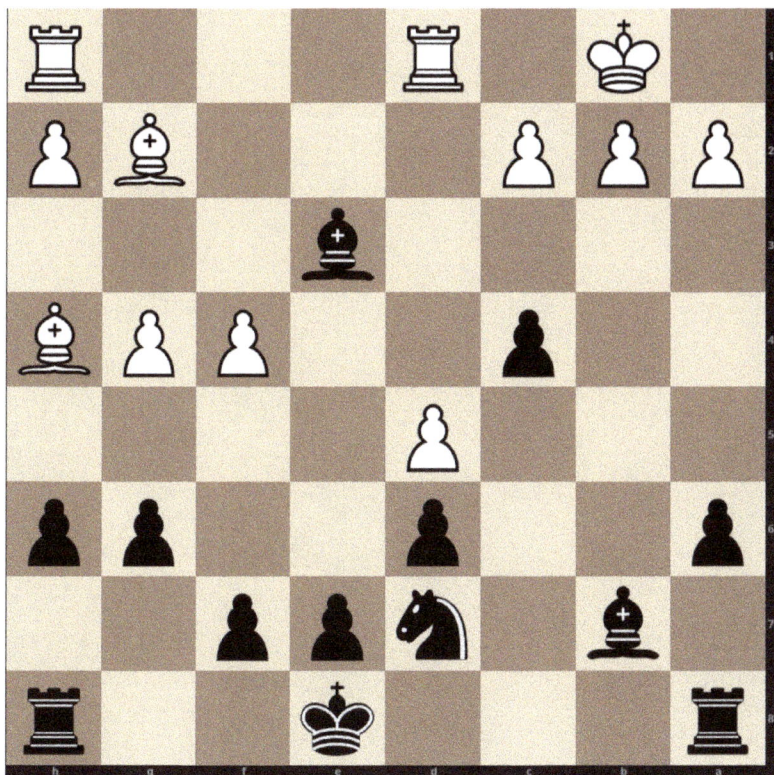

Fig. 75

19. It's white to play. There is a continuation for white that leads to material advantage. You need to check all variations and find the best one.

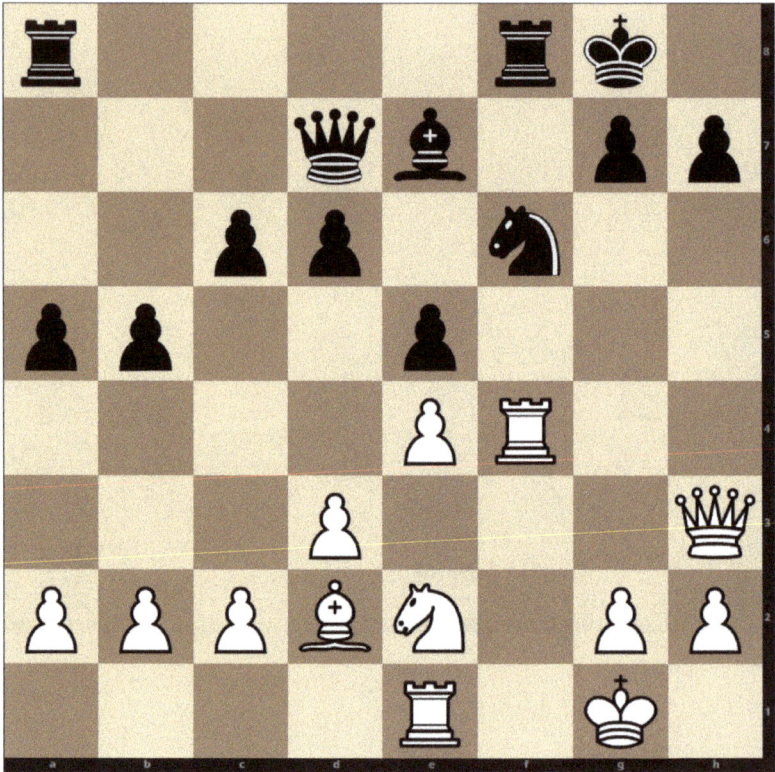

Fig. 76

Rxf6 removes the defender of the black queen, hence forcing black's next move: Qxh3

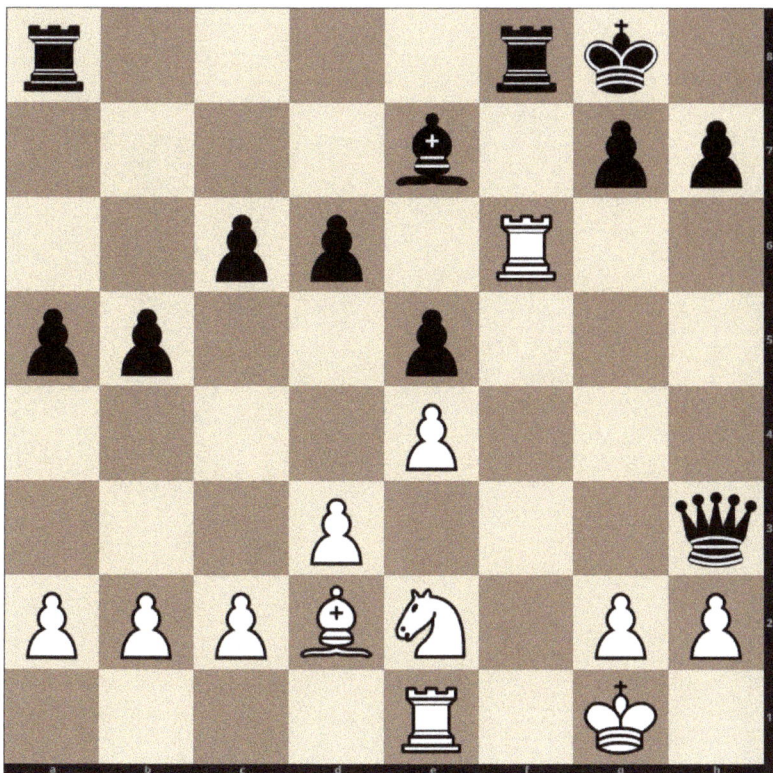

Fig. 77

Now black has a forcing in-between move: Rxf8+ which forces black to take back.

Fig. 78

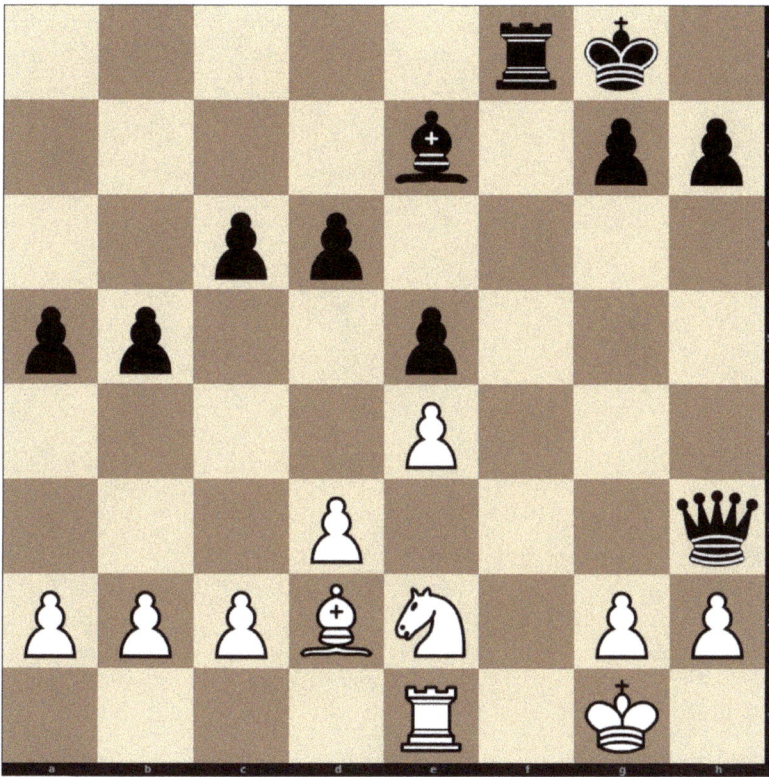

Fig. 79

Now white can cash-in by finally taking the queen.

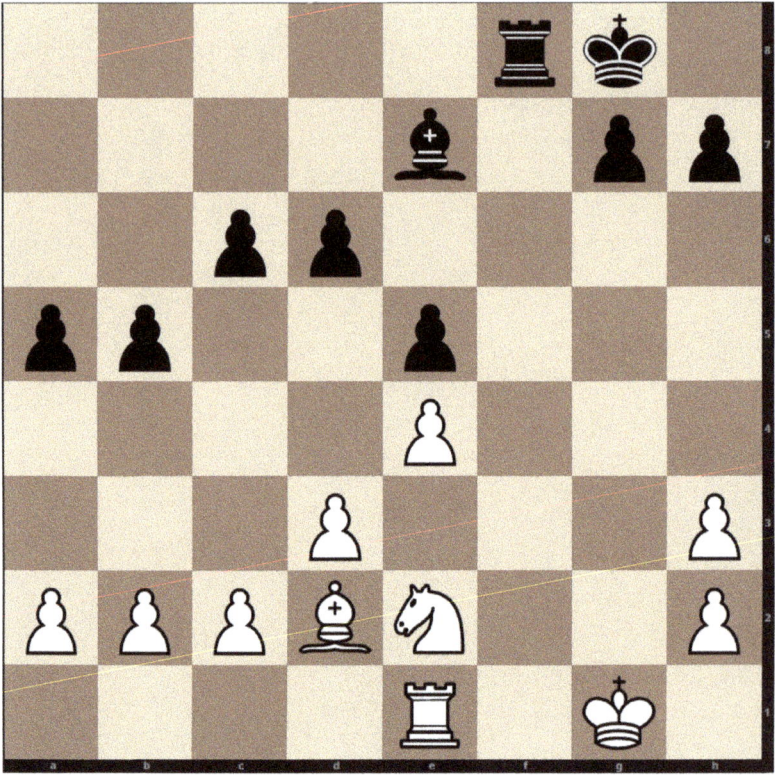

Fig. 80

White is up a piece and should be winning the game if played solidly from here.

20. In the position below it's white to play. White shouldn't think superficially and think about moving the knight on b5 back because it's threatened.

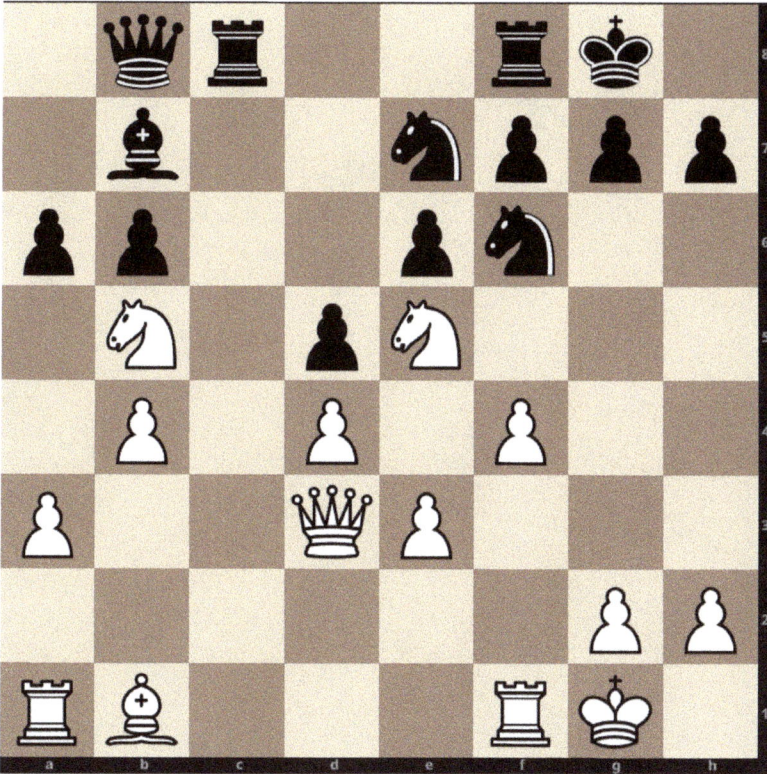

Fig. 81

White has an active threat to checkmate on h7 with the battery of white square bishop and the queen. The only piece defending the mate threat on h7 is the knight on f6. Does white have a move to deflect the only defender of the checkmate? Yes, Nd7.

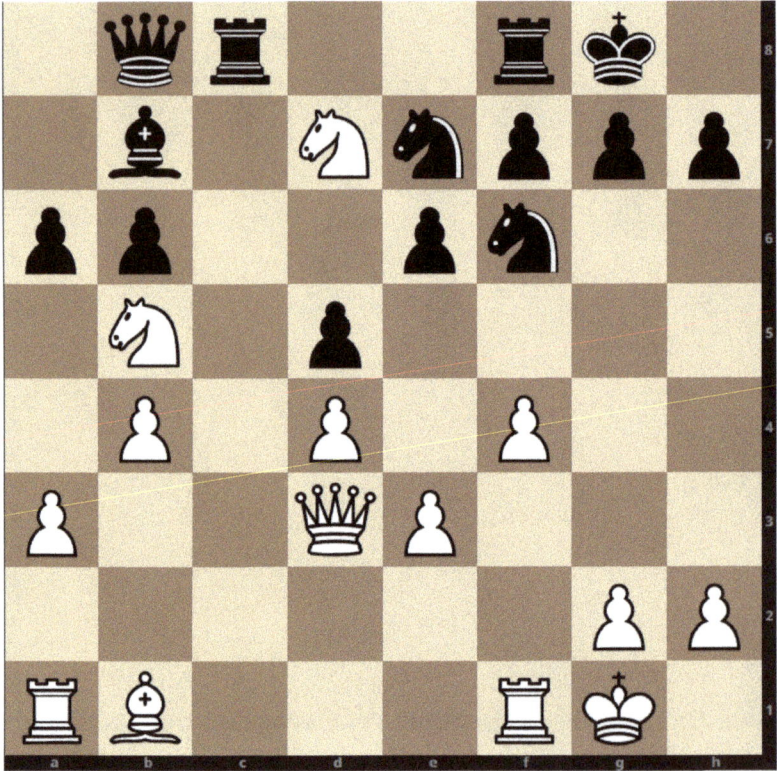

Fig. 82

This move can not be ignored by black, otherwise next move white will take the knight on f6 and then checkmate on h7 would be unavoidable no matter what black plays next. Black is forced to react to the checkmate threat by blocking the queen's path to checkmate with Nf5 or Ng6.

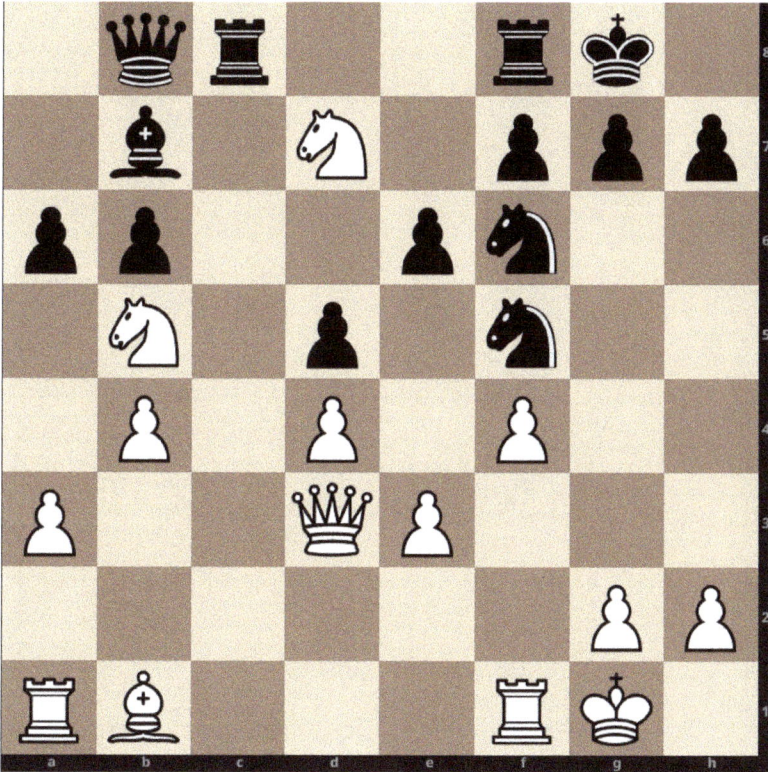

Fig. 83

Unfortunately mate threat can not be parried without giving up the queen on b8. Next move white will take the queen with the knight and eventually win the game with serious material advantage.

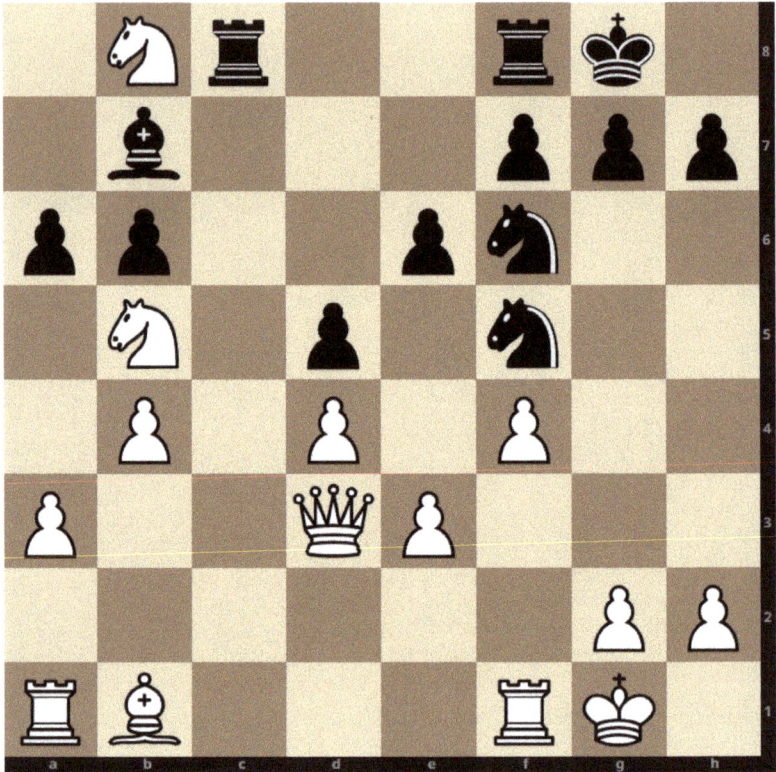

Fig. 84